60 SECONDS AND YOU'RE HIRED

60 SECONDS AND YOU'RE HIRED

Robin Ryan, M.Ed.

IMPACT PUBLICATIONS
Manassas Park, VA

Library of Congress Cataloguing-in-Publication Data

Ryan, Robin, 1955—
   60 seconds and you're hired! / Robin Ryan.
     p. cm.
   Inlcudes bibliographical references and index.
   ISBN 1-57023-009-9 : $9.95
   1. Employment interviewing. I. Title. II. Title: Sixty seconds and you're hired!
HF5549.5.I6R94   1994
650.14—dc20   94—458
                                              CIP

For information on distribution or quantity discount rates, Tel. 703/361-7300, Fax 703/355-9486, or write to: Sales Department, IMPACT Publications, 9104-N Manassas Drive, Manassas Park, VA 22111. Distributed to the trade by National Book Network, 4720 Boston Way, Suite A, Lanham, MD 20706, Tel. 301/459-8696.

CONTENTS

ACKNOWLEDGEMENTS

In my efforts to share my information to aid you in your job search, several key people need to be thanked for their help and support. A big thank you to every job hunter who has worked with me or who has attended my seminars. They are why I wrote this book and helping them is the driving force in my life. I would like to thank Tracy White, who started my seminar business years ago when she first hired me to teach job hunting skills to the CPA's. Her continued support and assistance has been an important contribution in my career. I would also like to thank Henriette Klauser, who shared her knowledge and encouragement on writing a book and gave me direction when I needed it, as well as, Cindy Jackson, who translated my written words and quickly typed each page of this manuscript. Thanks go to Cindy Hurst, Mike Hurst, Steve Ryan, Jim Mullen and Sandy DeHan — who all willingly read this book and offered valuable insights to improve it. I'm grateful to KIRO TV and Radio for their continuous support and endorsement. Lastly, I'm grateful to my parents for raising me to believe that any goal is possible if you have a burning desire to achieve it.

DEDICATION

To my husband Steven —

You always used to say *I was the best job getter you know*. Your support and encouragement has been vital in my mission to share information with others.

May they find a career as rewarding as mine.

*Believing in yourself
is the starting point.
Effectively communicating
your abilities to
others is the necessity.*

1

WHY 60 SECONDS?

"We would like you to come in for an interview." Every job hunter wants to hear those wonderful words and once they do, they begin forming a vision of landing the job. When you get that call you hang up the phone, excited and pleased that your resume has gotten you this far.

On the other end of the phone sits the employer who decided to call you for an interview. Three thoughts run through his mind — Can you do the job? Will you do the job? Will you fit into their organization? The employer worries about not being able to find a good person to do their job. The workload is piling up; the pressure is on to make a good hiring decision. The employer hopes that you'll be "the one." The employer thinks about the important job duties he needs done. He's feeling anxious, hopeful, skeptical all at once. He's hoping you have the skills to do the job.

For the employer, hiring is a difficult task. Mistakes can be very costly. Employee turnover often costs one-third of a person's salary, when adding in the loss of work, expense of errors, and training a new person. The employer wants to find the right person — quickly. He looks for someone who can and will do his job well. He looks for an answer to the problem of whom to hire.

To convince this employer, there are compelling reasons why the 60 Seconds approach is the ideal way to get your points across.

1

In today's fast paced world, we often focus on things for less than 60 seconds. Verbose, lengthy answers — where job hunters babble on and on when answering interview questions — bore the interviewer into not hiring them. Nervousness and no preparation often result in long, continuous, never-ending answers.

The most effective way to capture attention is to use your enthusiasm to answer each question succinctly in a concise, brief manner. And never use more than 60 seconds on any answer.

ARE THEY LISTENING?

Job hunters are amazed to learn that interviewers can ask them 60 minutes worth of questions and never hear any of the answers. Why? Because they aren't listening. They are tired, distracted, bored, and feel the candidate is the wrong choice — that they can't do the job. When you get your point across in 60 seconds or less, you increase the odds that the person will listen. When you add specifics of how you've accomplished the needed tasks before, show support materials and work examples, add vocal variety and enthusiasm to your answers, the employer starts to wake up and take notice. And when you put into practice your 5 Point Agenda and 60 Second Sell, the whole process takes on a new shape in which the employer begins to get *excited* that they may have found the right person for the job — YOU!

THE WORLD IS FULL OF SOUND BITES

Television and radio have filled our world with 30 and 60 second commercials — short, concise commercials that quickly get their point across. News reports use the same principles; limiting stories to short one to three minute segments. We are all conditioned to these speedy communication tools. During a job interview, utilizing the right words that effectively get your message across concisely will build the employer's confidence that you can do the job.

YOUR VERBAL BUSINESS CARD

The 60 Second Sell is your basic tool to create interest on the part of the employer. This 60 second calling card will summarize your skills, abilities, and previous experience in a well thought out fashion that will immediately make the employer want to listen. The 60 Second Sell is a proven shortcut to your success. It's easy to create and very easy to use. Once you've learned this technique, your interviews will be greatly improved because you'll do the most important thing necessary to land a job — you get the employer to listen to you.

2

5 POINT AGENDA

The 5 Point Agenda is a solution to break through the monotony, the disinterest, and get the employer to listen. It is a hiring strategy created to fit the needs of the employer and the job to be done. The 5 Point Agenda is a predetermined analysis in which you select your five most marketable points and repeatedly weave these points throughout the interview process. It is this repetition and reiteration of exactly how you'll meet their needs that allows the employer to remember something about you. Clients have tested this interview approach with the following results:

1. It made interview preparation easier.
2. They were highly rated by everyone who interviewed them.
3. The 5 Points seemed to be all that were remembered.
4. They credited the 5 Point Agenda and the 60 Second Sell as the two techniques that secured the job offer.

Job hunters are often amazed to learn that an interviewer can ask you an entire hour of questions and not hear one word you've said. They become bored with the process or you create the wrong image so they don't tune in. After interviewing several people, everyone begins to blend together. I experience this when I hire people and countless other employers have confirmed this. The 5 Point Agenda captures their interest because you are continually emphasizing exactly how you *can* do their job.

THE FORMULA FOR
CREATING YOUR STRATEGY

Examine your previous experience. Write out the major responsibilities for each job you've held. Note any special accomplishments. Zero in on your important work strengths — those abilities where you are most productive.

Check with your contacts and network to get as much background information on the employer as possible. Thoroughly examine all the information you've been able to obtain about the employer and the position's needs. Many times, your contacts will point out the very aspects that must make up your 5 Point Agenda. Other times, there will be little information available and you will need to guess based on what you know about doing that job in general.

After reviewing the employer and position needs, determine which parts of your abilities and experience will be most important *to the employer*. Then create your 5 Point Agenda, selecting each point to build a solid picture emphasizing how you *can* do their job.

THREE EXAMPLES

Let's examine three 5 Point Agendas that clients used during the interview process to land their new jobs. The jobs they applied for were: Chief Financial Officer, Events Planner, and Engineer.

Chief Financial Officer

This position was with a rapidly expanding international company needing strong financial and operations management.

- Point 1 — 15 years in senior financial management, directing international business start-ups, expansions, and turn-arounds.
- Point 2 — Took start-up manufacturer from zero to $38 million in 18 months.
- Point 3 — Achieved corporate profitability goals at last 5

positions, exceeded goals at 4.
- Point 4 — Hired over 3500+ employees, uniting diverse workforce into cohesive productive teams.
- Point 5 — Management Information System expertise in hardware, software, network conversions, transportation/ accounting/distribution systems.

It's important to note that the last point was simply a guess at the company's perceived need. During the interview process, this client realized that computer systems were a crucial need for this employer and was able to offer specific examples of his experience in this management information system area and noted the results positively affected the company's bottom line.

Events Planner

The association needed a person with strong computer and desktop publishing skills and previous events planning experience. As a new college grad, the applicant created her 5 Point Agenda from her internship and part time jobs:

- Point 1 — Proficient IBM and Macintosh computer skills.
- Point 2 — Desktop publishing using Pagemaker, creating brochures, programs, invitations, flyers, press releases and training materials.
- Point 3 — Assisted with numerous special events, conferences, lunches, receptions.
- Point 4 — Responsible for catering, food preparation, audio visual set up, transportation, budget, expense reimbursements.
- Point 5 — Acquired service bids from several contractors, caterers, hotels.

Engineer

This major automotive manufacturer required experience in both quality assurance and new product design. The applicant's 5 Point Agenda was:

- Point 1 — Implemented new four year quality assurance program which received a national Quality-1 Award.

- Point 2 — Effectively dealt with employee resistance to quality improvements.
- Point 3 — Conducted 37 suppliers on-site inspections to improve the quality of parts received.
- Point 4 — Five years design engineering experience.
- Point 5 — Excellent communication skills when working with both technical and non technical staff.

The 5 points are your basic building blocks to answer the interviewer's questions. You want to re-stress each of these points whenever the opportunity presents itself. The message the employer hears contains your solid, most marketable skills affecting your ability to do the job.

3

60 SECOND SELL

The 60 Second Sell is a tool that helps you target the employer's needs. It allows you to summarize your most marketable strengths in a brief and concise manner. Successful job hunters report that the 60 Second Sell is the most influential tool they use during the interview process. They praise the tool for several reasons:

1. It is effective in capturing the employer's attention.
2. It provide an excellent concise answer to tricky questions.
3. It is very easy to use the formula.
4. It is a great way to end an interview.

The 60 Second Sell is a 60 second memorized statement that summarizes and links together your 5 Point Agenda. You will order your ideas so that the thoughts flow in the most effective way. You should be able to convey the ideas you link together in 60 seconds or less. Once you learn this technique it will be easy for you to recall and use during the interview.

Although you should memorize the ideas, do not feel you must use exactly the same words to convey your thoughts each time. This should sound natural rather than memorized.

WHEN TO USE IT

Certain questions can cause job hunters to flounder and babble. In one interview I conducted, I asked a very typical interview question, "Tell me about yourself." I got a 20 minute answer. I immediately imagined this person in an executive meeting — the meeting might never end. Had the person answered with a 60 Second Sell, he might have begun the interview with me listening and interested. Questions such as "Tell me about yourself" require a brief summary, not a life story. Other questions in which your 60 Second Sell is the perfect answer include: "Why should I hire you?" which is asking you to convince the employer to hire you, What are your strengths? What makes you think you are qualified for this job? What makes you think you will succeed in this position? Why do you want this job?" These questions offer you an excellent way to use your 60 Second Sell. The preface will vary depending on which question you are answering. To respond to "Why do you want this job?" begin with "It's important I use my strengths and I feel that _(your 60 Second Sell)_ would be assets when performing your job."

The 60 Second Sell is effective because it demonstrates your strengths and illustrates how you will fill the employer's needs. That is the key to its success.

THREE EXAMPLES

To show you how your 5 Point Agenda is linked and becomes your 60 Second Sell, let's continue with our three earlier examples starting with their 5 Point Agendas. Here is how their points were linked together to summarize and create their 60 Second Sell.

Chief Financial Officer

This international company was in a rapid expansion phase that required expertise in financial as well as operational management. His 60 Second Sell stressed how he'd accomplished it before:

"I have 15 years in senior financial management directing business expansions, start-ups and turnarounds in the international arena. In my last three positions, I achieved all corporate profitability goals and exceeded goals in four of those situations. For example, I took a start up manufacturer from zero to $38 million in 18 months.

I base my success on two abilities. The first is my ability to hire excellent people and build a cohesive productive team and the second is my Management Information System expertise. I've hired over 3500+ employees and using job accountability and training achieved highly productive bottom line results. I used my computer expertise to select hardware, software, transportation, and distribution; accounting systems to analyze and streamline costs; and put in place the most effective safeguard systems that will maximize profits. I've always produced measurable bottom line results and feel that I would produce the same for you."

Events Planner

When interviewing for an Events Coordinator position with heavy computer and desktop publishing skills, our new grad said:

"I have assisted with numerous special events during the last two years — planning conferences, receptions, lunches and dinners. I've been responsible for all the details, the facilities, catering and lodging arrangements, equipment and food set-ups, taking care of the transportation needs plus handling expenses and vouchers. I have learned to make any budget work. By being resourceful I was able to work within budget limitations. I have had a great deal of experience comparing and selecting service contractors such as caterers and facilities.

My computer strengths have been most beneficial to my previous employer. I have extensive IBM and Macintosh experience and easily use Pagemaker to create brochures, flyers, program schedules, invitations, and training materials. It is both the experience in event planning and my computer skills that would be assets to you in this position."

Engineer

When interviewing with the major automotive manufacturer for a Quality Assurance Engineer position, his 60 Second Sell went something like this:

"For my last employer I implemented a new quality assurance program for seven plants over a four year period. We received the Q-1 award for our efforts. Along the way, I've learned to effectively deal with employee resistance to quality improvements through training, selling the teamwork concepts and utilizing a personal empowerment approach. I have evaluated 37 suppliers during on-site inspections to improve the quality of their product — parts that will ultimately become a piece of my company's final product. My five years in design engineering, coupled with strong communication skills, has aided me in my ability to work with a diverse population and solve technical problems. These are the reasons I feel I would be a valuable contributor to your company."

Both the 60 Second Sell and the 5 Point Agenda must be created for *each* interview. They may vary slightly or greatly based on what you determine to be that employer's most important needs and your most marketable abilities to meet those needs.

4

60 SECOND ANSWERS TO TOUGH, TRICKY QUESTIONS

There are two key components to successfully answering interview questions: advance preparation and short, concise, specific answers that never exceed 60 Seconds. Answers to even the toughest questions will be easier to handle when you've thought about them and jotted down answers before the interview starts.

In order to help you prepare, I've answered 80 tough, tricky questions including the typical ones you'll most likely to be asked. Knowing how to answer the employer's questions is vital to your success. Your self-confidence is dependent on knowing you can effectively answer questions that demonstrate to the employer you can do their job. I'll show where to use examples that reiterate your 5 Point Agenda and where to use your 60 Second Sell.

Short, concise answers that encourage a conversation and exchange of information is the goal. Employers know that nervousness can cause job hunters to babble endlessly to each question. Demonstrate your self-confidence and retain their interest with short, effective answers. Too often job hunters answer a question, pause, get nervous and add more information which takes away from the initial answer.

Review the explanations and answers below, then choose your own words and formulate your answers to potential questions. The result — you'll be prepared to handle any question concisely, getting your point across in 60 seconds or less.

1. "Why did you leave your last job?"

Good reasons to depart include: want more challenge or growth opportunities, relocation, layoffs, reorganization or downsizing which affected your duties. A typical answer might be, "The company is downsizing and I recognized that there will be no growth opportunities for me." Another answer might be, "My current employer is small and I've gone as far as I can with their organization. I'm looking for a challenge that will really use my abilities and strengths to make a contribution." A different response could be, "We've just relocated to this area to be near our family, and that's why I'm available."

2. "Tell me about your proudest accomplishments."

Review your 60 Second Sell and 5 Point Agenda. Think about what you're trying to stress, and **then** write down three big work-related accomplishments that demonstrate your ability to do the employer's job. Employment, community or association work can often be examined to find just the right example to make your point.

3. "Describe your ideal supervisor."

This is really saying, "Can you work with me?" Frame your answer accordingly. Point out the type of management style that allows you to be the most productive on the job.

4. "Describe the worst supervisor you've ever had."

As much as you want to criticize an old boss and point out that person's faults, I suggest you reconsider. It will reflect negatively on you. Instead try this, "One boss didn't give me very much feedback. In fact, I only heard from him when there was a problem. Months might go by without any kind of feedback or idea of what he was thinking. Although I don't like to have someone standing over my shoulder, I do like to have input, exchange ideas and get a feel that my work is in line with my boss and the company's goals. Open communication I guess is what was lacking. I think that's really important between me and my supervisor." This answer demonstrates a positive response on how teamwork is important in achieving the employer's goals.

5. "What features of your previous job did you like?"

When you talk about things that you like, relate them to the job you're going to do for this potential employer. Talk specifically about things that they're going to have you do in their job, such as publish the newsletter, or operate a computer system.

6. "What features of your last job did you dislike?"

This is a tricky one. Be sure you point out something that won't affect your ability to do their job. When you select an example use information you know about the new job, such as all this company's publications are printed out of house. At your old job, everything was done in-house. So you might answer with, "One of the things I really disliked was the length of time needed to complete printing projects. We did things in-house; many times everything was backed-up several weeks. I found it frustrating to need seven weeks to get a project that could have been turned around at a commercial printing place within five days. I felt the process was not very productive or effective."

7. "What is your greatest weakness?"

If you think about this in advance and you have a written-out answer, it's really not that tough of a question. I recommend that you pick something that has nothing to do with your ability to accomplish their job. An answer that I've always used was, "Well I'm not very mechanical, so when the copy machine breaks down, you better not call me." Ha, ha, ha, joke, joke, joke. A little humor in the interview is definitely okay. And often we would go on to the next question. But if they came back and said, "No, now really, what is your greatest weakness?" I might say, "Well you know, sometimes when I'm working on a project I just get so absorbed, I forget to look at the time. Before you know, the time to leave has long gone by and I'm still there. I guess that's a weakness, I guess I should realize that you should be able to leave right at five. But when I'm working on a project and I'm being creative, and things are rolling, I just stay on until I can get it done." Here a weakness is turned into a positive, appealing trait. Try to choose something that's not going to "hurt" your chances of getting hired. Another alternative is to say "I have excellent computer user skills. I know Excel and WordPerfect inside and out, but I am pretty weak at actual programming and would need more training if I were to write your software programs." Since programming software is not necessary to doing this job, it is a moot point. With advance thought you can choose something similar that will have no direct impact on the hiring decision.

8. "What are your strengths?"

You respond with your 60 Second Sell. Tailor it to the particular needs of this job.

9. "Describe a time when you were criticized for poor performance."

This question is a mine field. You must use a specific incident, yet carefully choose an example that you can demonstrate what you did to correct the situation. Selecting an example, such as poor computer skills, allowing you to continue on to say that you enrolled in a class and after several months you are now quite proficient. This demonstrates your abilities to take constructive criticism and improve. Avoid answers that deal with late arrivals, absenteeism, or interpersonal conflicts as these often send red flag warnings to an employer about your dependability and ability to fit into an organization.

10. "I'm a little worried abut your lack of . . ."

If the employer is unaware of your experience such as computer skills, then it's easy to give an answer using an example. "At my old company, I was responsible for a lot of the data entry. I used a mainframe with customized software. I have a natural aptitude for computers and would be willing to spend lunch hours and some evenings on my own time learning your software so I can come up to speed quickly."

If they are concerned about a skill you do lack, but are eager to learn, try "I appreciate your honesty. I have excellent customer services skills, but you are right, I have not been a sales person. I do know the key to success is building good client relationships, persistence, using good time management skills and learning the trade. I have read numerous books on selling and understand the process. I will take seminars at my own expense to learn everything I can about selling. I am a hard worker, who lets rejection roll off my back. My goals include landing a sales job and then becoming one of the top sales people in my company. I've set a three year date to achieve this goal. I'm determined to succeed."

11. "You have a lot of experience. Why would you want this job?"

The employer fears you are over qualified and will get bored and want to leave their job quickly if they hire you. You have anticipated this question. Do not oversell your abilities. Do not show you are desperate, that you'll take *any* job. Remember the employer wants you to want *their* job, not *a* job. Stress why this job fits for you now. Talk about life changes, need for more structure, desire to make a long term contribution. Be careful not to say you want an easy, no stress job, causing the employer to doubt whether you would continue to do the work they need done.

12. "Describe a difficult co-worker you've had to deal with."

Careful, we are looking for turf wars, troublesome employees, and any red flags you care to raise. Try to show a misunderstanding and your efforts to correctly resolve it. "I dealt with the engineering manager who is often blunt and can hurt other's feelings. He was always sharp with my assistant and one day was particularly so over a report he needed. As she was greatly upset, I decided to discuss what was becoming a problem. I approached it from his perspective, a visual, analytical thinker. I asked him to write me when requesting reports and to state the day and time he needed them so that I could assure him he'd get them on time. I then mentioned that my assistant was a very competent, but very sensitive person. And that yesterday he had upset her and that I would appreciate his help in dealing with her. I proceeded to brainstorm with him on ways we could all improve to work together."

Here you've pointed out a problem and the solution of working together and asking for input. Open minded, but also responding to your staff's needs. Select an example that demonstrates your ability to effectively work out differences with co-workers.

13. "Describe how you work under pressure, deadlines, etc."

The interviewer is interested in your time management skills, and workload organization. A good response might be "I try to plan all major projects in a reverse time line. I start with the deadline and work backwards to set divisional deadlines for the pieces of the project. I work well under pressure. I have always made deadlines in the past. I use time management and planning grids, to do lists, project scheduling, plus spread sheets. These tools help me to best utilize my time and to avoid becoming frantic and overloaded as the last hours of a deadline draw near."

14. "What do you know about our company?"

"That I could be a strong contributor that you need . . ." and then go into your 60 Second Sell.

15. "What two or three things are most important to you in your job?"

Select two or three points from your 5 Point Agenda and frame your answer to say "It's important that I use my skills to be a productive contributor to my company. I believe when I'm using my computer abilities and negotiation skills, I'm working at my best. That's important to me." Be sure to select two or three items essential to doing the employer's job successfully.

16. "Why did you change jobs so frequently?"

Job hopping is more common in the 90's as we have become a more mobile society. Dual career families are often relocating with the spouse's job history showing numerous changes. Often the truth works best. If you have moved a lot, try "My husband's position required us to move quite often. His last promotion here guaranteed that we would remain in the area permanently. I'm eager to get my career on track and bring long term contributions to my employer. On the various jobs, I have developed excellent accounting skills, used numerous software programs and quickly become a productive worker."

Or if the job changes came from obtaining better positions say: "Each position allowed me to learn new skills and every job was on a promotional path. Most have been with very small companies, where leaving was the only option for advancement."

17. "What do you think of your previous boss?"

If you loved your boss, this is an easy one. If you found your boss difficult to work with, be careful when phrasing your answer. Negative comments can send up a red flag of a problem employee. Resist the urge to bad mouth your boss. Try "My boss had extensive experience in the field and I learned a lot working under him." or "My boss had an open door policy and was very approachable. I found this to be an asset in our working relationship."

18. "This is a very high pressured job. Do you think you're up to it?"

The only way to prove you can handle pressure is to give an example. Sales, customer service, operations, top management positions often get this question. Create an example like this "Cabinet sales is a high pressure business. Our margins are tight and we constantly need new business. Last year we opened a new territory and the heat was on for us to produce. I met with my sales team and we established new goals. I let them pick the reward structure that motivated them. Most choose a paid vacation, not higher commissions. So, every week I sent a note with a picture of their goal — Hawaii scenes, a freshly painted house, dollar bills — to keep up the momentum. It worked and the entire department was rewarded for surpassing corporate's goals."

19. "Why do you want to leave your present job?"

Companies want to hear that you seek more challenge, more advancement, a promotion, more financial reward. You can also leave to shorten your commute or because your company is unstable. Answer with "I have learned so much working for a small company, but there are no promotional opportunities. I enjoy challenges and learning new skills as well as improving my old ones. Therefore, I seek a new position at this time." Or "I noticed that your company had an opening. I've been very happy at my present position, but the option to move to a good company, such as yours, and only have a ten minute commute is very appealing. Right now I commute 45 minutes to an hour each way." Or, for a small company, try "I've gained a lot of experience at my other positions. But now I want an opportunity for more responsibility, to have greater impact on the end results. Your company will really allow me to see the fruits of my labor and that is important to me."

20. "Do you mind routine work?"

The key here is to recognize that routine work is the job. Your answer should be "I enjoy structure; it allows me to be efficient in doing the tasks correctly."

21. "Have you ever been asked to resign?"

The answer to this question is "no." You were either fired, laid off, or you choose to quit. You may have been presented with the option of leaving, but you still choose to leave. Too many lawsuits have been initiated over this issue. Your former employer would not likely admit to forcing you out. Therefore, honestly say "no."

22. "Tell me about one of your failures."

This is a very tricky question. I suggest you answer by giving an example of a set-back or a learning experience and show what you did to improve. "I decided that our company would benefit by having a lunch time brown bag training program. I lined up some speakers, scheduled the room and sent out a notice. Four people showed out of 800. The next drew three people. I had failed, but I couldn't understand why. I asked numerous employees and kept hearing the topics *were* of interest. Most wanted to know what they'd learn and wanted a relaxed, fun setting. I asked a friend in marketing who suggested using a snappy title for the program and each seminar. Changing the copy and using graphics did the trick. During a recent company survey, the luncheon program was rated as an important benefit and drew 75 to 80 employees per meeting. You see, I believe there aren't failures, only learning experiences, which is what I experienced here."

23. "We work a lot of late nights here. Is that going to cause any trouble at home?"

"I am able and willing to work whatever hours you need me. I expected that with this position evenings would be necessary, as they were in my previous position." Reassure the employer that you will work the hours they need. Your reliability and dependability is what they are questioning.

24. "You have too much experience for this job. Why would you want it?"

Employers are reluctant to hire a person who is overqualified because the person is unlikely to be happy, stay long, or be seriously interested just in doing the job hired for. They do not want someone who is burnt out and sees their job as an easy paycheck. Often you can be threatening to the interviewer, especially if you are truly suited for the interviewer's job. Examine why you want the position. "I need a job" is not a response that will endear you to them. You must use your acting skills to convince them why a demotion is a good option. Try: "My current position as controller requires ten nights of travel per month. This has become an increasingly difficult sacrifice for my family. I have decided to seek an accounting position that allows me to focus on my strengths — taxes, audits and computer integration — but that allows me to go home each evening. The subsidiary I work for is typical of similar companies in our industry — the controller position requires a lot of out-of-town travel to do the job. I believe the financial skills I bring will benefit your organization and I see this as a win/win situation for both of us." Create a reasonable explanation. Showing desperation and being willing to take any job often makes the interviewer disqualify you. They need that job done and you must show you can do it, but also that you *want* to do it.

25. "You've been with the same company for so many years, how will you cope with a new one?"

The interviewer is concerned that you'll be slow to adapt and change. Dispel that. "I have always been flexible and adaptable in taking on new tasks. I pride myself on being a constant learner. You'd benefit from my —." Use your 60 Second Sell to point out the experience you'd bring.

26. "What was it about your last job that bothered you the most?"

Here the interviewer is looking for incompatibles between what you dislike and aspects of their job. The best way to answer this is to select something that is either neutral or that would be a benefit. For example, "At my old company we had a very slow computer and a Pagemaker program that was two versions old. It took a lot of extra time and had less capabilities than the newest additions. I found it bothersome, but my old company didn't have the funds to update their equipment. As the editor of my association's newsletter, I used top of the line equipment like you have here and it made for a higher quality, faster produced product. I'd look forward to using your equipment each day."

27. "What motivates you?"

"Using my strengths and abilities to be a highly productive employee. I take pride in my work and am most motivated when I use my

_____ skills." Fill in that blank, naming some of the skills in your 5 Point Agenda.

28. "How creative a problem solver are you?"

This question is very tricky in that you aren't sure what the employer is getting at. You also want to know if there are big problems in which not enough funds and resources are available to fix. Therefore, I recommend you answer with a question to quantify what's being asked. Try "In the past, I've been a resourceful problem solver. Could you be more specific about the types of problems I'll need to solve here and I can give you examples of what I've done in the past." Be sure to get a good answer at some point in the hiring process about the company's stability and depth of problems it faces.

29. "Describe a large mistake you made at your last job."

Select an example that demonstrates a learning experience, and shows how you corrected the mistake. You might say something like: "I was under very tight deadlines and we had a large volume of work to get done. I only glanced at some important letters my assistant had done and signed the letters. Unfortunately, the meeting time and location were incorrect. It was embarrassing and required time I didn't have to call the 20 individuals and correct the error, but that's what I did. I smoothed it over, but my boss noticed and spoke to me about it. I sat down with my assistant and calmly discussed how we could prevent these errors in the future. Together we decided that we would read the information to the other and triple check to verify dates, times, locations. We decided to try to re-plan our work time to be less pushed at the last minute to catch the day's mail. I volunteered to bring the mail to the post office so not to have to rush and get everything done before our 1:00 mail pick up. This also helped decrease the pressure and eliminate mistakes made in haste." Here you've stressed teamwork, gaining staff cooperation and problem solving. To err is human, but it is the SOLUTIONS that you employ to fix or eliminate errors that matters to an employer.

30. "How would you describe your ideal job?"

State that your ideal job is one that uses your talents and allows you to be most productive. Mention several of your strengths from your 5 Point Agenda. The tendency for most job hunters is to get into elaborate discussions here about what they want — salary, benefits, work environment — and not focus on doing the employer's job. Save the salary and benefits discussions until after they make the offer. For now, you need to still convince them you're the right one for the job.

31. "How do you think your present/last boss would describe you?"

Whether you and your boss like each other is not the issue. Simply fall back on your 5 Point Agenda and describe your work. Mention three or four points that your boss would note that are important to doing this employer's job. If you plan to use your boss as a reference, it makes a very strong statement if you end with this phrase, "My boss will be happy to verify this, feel free to call her."

32. "How would you rate yourself as a leader? A supervisor? An employee?"

Analytical individuals often rate themselves low because they look to improve everything, including themselves and that is not a good approach here. Start with the employee part first. You could say, "I'm a highly regarded employee because I'm productive and good at what I do." If you are a supervisor and manager, continue on to say "I treat everyone fairly and that allows me to have a good working relationship with my staff. I'm approachable, but also hold each person accountable for doing their job well and achieving the department's goals. In the past, my department has always been recognized for its productivity under my leadership." You can say this even if you've won no awards. All departments have goals and if you achieve yours then it signifies you are in sync with the company's demands.

33. "You've worked for yourself now for awhile so why do you want to work for our company?"

The truth is that self employment is hard work. It takes endless hours, excellent business operation knowledge, capital, marketing skills, and perseverance to survive. Four out of five small businesses fail. The employer doesn't want an employee who is burned out and wants an easy paycheck. And life changes — a divorce, ill spouse — often create the need for a steady income and company benefits. Think through the answer and then respond honestly. "I really am at my best training employees. I get outstanding evaluations and work hard to create an effective learning environment. I found that as a consultant at least 40% of my time was spent on marketing and business development. I failed to make follow-up calls because I would rather rework and improve my curriculum. I found I disliked 'selling' so I made a decision to seek employment. The job I really want is to spend all my time training others. Your company's position allows me to use my strengths as a trainer and focus on just that — training."

34. "Give me an example of a time you had to deal with criticism from your boss."

No one likes to be criticized. Truth is, most of us will get a little hurt, maybe angry, definitely defensive. To answer this question, it is best to point out an idea that was criticized, or work that you corrected and improved. Your answer can cause the interviewer to question your ability to do their job. You could give an example such as "I remember a time that I was a rather new employee in a meeting of all the department managers. We discussed increasing the company's visibility among potential customers. My idea was to advertise in a certain magazine. I was heavily criticized by two other department heads. I kept cool, restated my reasons that were clear to me, but not to them. Unfortunately, I had no research or data to back up the validity of my idea when I first mentioned it. After the meeting, I wrote out the idea and noted some of our own market research that supported the idea. I then sent it along to the sales manager. Months passed and a competitor used my idea as part of their advertising campaign. My boss and the sales manager both re-evaluated the input and I believe I gained more respect with the department for my ideas after that. But, I also learned that the executive committee likes substantiated data, so now I prepare the supporting rationale before I present the idea."

If you select an example about your work needing improvement, demonstrate the steps you took to correct the situation. "I gave a presentation to our executive group. I was nervous and not prepared for all the questions they asked. My boss pointed out several weak points about my presentation style. His feedback was hard to take at the time, but I followed up on his suggestions. I worked on my style — took a class and even had myself video taped. My boss's feedback was important in helping me improve my job performance. Employers want to hear that when their feedback is valid you'll take steps to improve your performance. These examples work very well to illustrate that point."

35. "What's the most difficult challenge you've faced in your life?"

You will need to discuss a specific example that demonstrates how tough the situation was and how you handled it. I often recommend you stick to work related situations. Avoid discussing co-worker problems unless you can show how you changed your approach or attitude to improve the working relationship. Personal tragedies are usually our most difficult challenges in life, but I feel that discussing them in an interview can cause extreme emotional reactions within you and thus create a problem for you in handling the rest of the interview with the employer. If you have ever had to fire someone, then use that experience. Everyone finds it difficult to take away a person's livelihood. State how you tried to improve the worker's performance, carefully considered the decision, and then, with professionalism, terminated the employee.

36. "What are you doing now to improve yourself?"

Employers value employees who believe in lifelong learning. It is best to note that you are taking a course or reading a book to gain or improve a skill. You could say "I joined Toastmasters three months ago to work on perfecting my public speaking skills" or "I presently am going to college at night to pursue a degree in business."

37. "How would you influence someone to accept your ideas?"

The interviewer is interested in evaluating the depth of your communication skills and persuading others. Try "I've learned that it is important to offer an idea using the right framework. It is important to look at who is the person or persons evaluating the idea and then determining the best approach that will appeal to them. I always have a rationale for why and how the idea will work. I try to think through the details beforehand. I'm open minded about the feedback my idea gets and look for ways to improve it or implement it so it will work."

38. "Could you explain in detail your experience with computer software programs?"

Be very specific in answering this question and be sure to ask what they use. You might say "Are you on an IBM system?" If they say yes, then go on to say "that's what we have now. I work mostly with two programs, WORD and EXCEL. I'm a very advanced user on WORD.

I can do mail mergers, use the tool box for charts and graphics. I use WORD everyday. On EXCEL I can create spreadsheet and formulas easily." This shows a high level user. If you know they have different software, you might continue to say "Lotus is a spreadsheet similar to EXCEL. I know all the Lotus concepts and feel it wouldn't take much time to become proficient in EXCEL. I would certainly be willing to put in some of my own time to speed up the learning process."

39. "Tell me about something your boss did that you disliked."

It's best not to criticize your boss, though noting something like "He smoked," if you are certain the interviewer does not, is okay. If not say, "We have a job to do and we all work together to do it well. I respect my boss and can't think of anything negative."

40. "How do you organize and plan for major projects?"

Stress in-depth planning and tracking, plus time management. "I use timelines, 'To Do' lists, responsibility charts, staff progress meetings, problem solving sessions and goal setting."

41. "What was the last book you read?"

Often this is a question to see what you read off the job. A common mistake is to select a current "hot" business book and drop that title. More often than not, the next questions will lead to an extensive discussion of that book's principles, theories and a defense of your opinions. So don't try to fake it to impress the interviewer — state a book you know well enough that you can talk about the plot or content.

42. "Tell us about a personal goal that you still want to achieve."

Share a goal that would increase your value as a worker. Cite a new skill — supervisor training, public speaking, a new computer software skill — that, once learned, increases your value to the employer. A specialized degree, such as an MBA, that you want to achieve can also be a good choice.

43. "Describe to me your typical work day."

Here the interviewer wants to know specifics to confirm you have handled most of their responsibilities before. Be sure to cover their most important duties in your answer, emphasizing the points in your 5 Point Agenda.

44. "Have you ever had any problems with poor attendance?"

If the answer is no, say "No, I haven't." This can easily be verified with references. If you have had a problem, then try to analyze what was the problem and offer a solution. Typical day care issues could be covered by saying, "when I was at ABC, my salary was lower then average which created difficulties in finding appropriate daycare. I often missed work when my child was sick because I could not afford a private sitter. I discussed this problem with my boss and my friends. I then decided that the situation wasn't fair to anyone. I asked my boss for a raise based on the quality of my work (which was high). He explained that the company had no budget for raises. I then decided to look for a new job. Since I've been at X Company, I've never missed a day. I have a good daycare situation that will take a sick child. I learned a lot about resourcefulness, and my value as a worker. I put 110% into my job and I know my current boss will attest to my productive levels and good attendance."

If illness was the reason you might say "Once I was dealing with a personal illness and was absent often over several weeks. It was completely resolved within three months and I'm quite healthy now and my most recent attendance has been excellent."

45. "Have you ever been responsible for managing financial budgets or department expenses?"

If the answer is yes, be specific. "Yes, I oversee my department's budget and approve all purchase orders and expenses. My budget is $100,000 annually and requires me to be resourceful and cautious in spending my department's funds." It is always good to add that you are cautious about spending someone else's money.

46. "What are the three most important responsibilities in your present job?"

Simply discuss the three areas that will be the most important to that employer in doing their job. Select them from your 5 Point Agenda.

47. "Tell me about an unpopular decision you had to make."

When you're in a position of responsibility you often have to make hard choices. Select a time where you chose the lesser of two evils or where you can provide solid explanations for a cost cutting measure. You could say "Our company was downsizing and we had to trim our labor costs. As the department manager, I selected dropping benefits and not terminating our employees. I sat down with the department and stated the problem and asked for their input. As a group, many wanted to fire the most recently hired. Unfortunately, these new employees and their jobs were critical to the company's future. I decided to eliminate all insurance benefits (life, dental, disability, and retirement) but retain the medical coverage with a small co-payment. Many of our longer term staff complained. I listened to them, but did what I felt served the company and department best."

Another option to use if you ever had to fire a well-liked person, you might say, "I had a very popular employee work for me who was ineffective and had low performance on her job. She was very friendly, but not able to learn the computer skills we needed. I elected to fire her. Many people complained all the way up to the CEO. They often admitted her work was inferior, but she was such a nice person I should not have fired her. Although my boss agreed with my choice, I took the heat and then carefully hired a new person who had the necessary skills. I purposely hired someone who would blend well with our other staff. In the end, it was the best thing for the department though personally difficult for me at the time."

48. "Give me an example of when it was necessary to reach a goal within a very short period of time and what you did to achieve it."

Select an example that demonstrates resourcefulness, adaptability and pitching in wherever necessary, such as: "The marketing department needed some data to produce a new brochure and we had three weeks to research, design, and write the new copy. Two days after we got the assignment, the sales department had secured a huge presentation to our most sought after client. They needed the brochure printed in ten days. Top priority. I reorganized my schedule and the graphic designer's. We forwarded calls to voice mail and within two days produced the copy and design needed to get the job done. The sales department made the pitch two days early and we landed a very big account as a result. I can't say it was the brochure that did it. I think it was the desire to win, to reach the goal, that inner motivation of being part of the team. We all worked very hard to get the results we wanted."

49. "Do you consider yourself successful?"

Of course you do. So answer "Yes, I do and I feel that my employer benefits because I always give 110% to my job, doing the very best I can."

50. "What would you do with an individual who is very angry and complaining to you?"

Think about what you do when faced with an angry person. Most angry people want someone to *listen* to their rage and *solve* their complaint. Often, just listening helps. Appropriate referrals or action steps to solve the problem might work also. Screaming, foul language might require you to request the person calm down and when they can more calmly explain the problem, you'll work on the solution. Your response to this question might be "Very angry, screaming people require a time-out, a cooling off period. I express this by telling them I can only listen if they are calm and want my help in finding a solution. I have found that listening often dissipates the anger. They want their problem fixed or solved. I know that dissatisfied customers often do a lot of damage, repeating their troubles to countless others. I do my best to find a workable solution that our organization can deal with and that will also satisfy the customer."

51. "Tell me about a time when your work performance was low."

Every job is affected by tragedies that happen in people's personal life. Select an example that deals with a short-lived personal crisis and show your efforts to deal with the issue to counteract your low performance. "I received some tragic news one morning that my brother was critically injured in a car crash. The workload was enormous and yet I could not really make the decisions necessary to run my department. I went to my boss and asked her to reassign some of my major responsibilities as I might need to fly across the country to be with my family. I told my staff my problem and asked for their help. My performance was below par all week. I did then leave for one week to attend the funeral. Upon my return, I took the time to write each staff person a note of thanks for all they did during this time. My staff was a stronger team as a result." This is a good example because you took responsibility to delegate your work and the situation was short lived. I suggest you avoid an answer such as this "I was going through a divorce and my work really suffered" response. Employers are not as sympathetic to long term poor performance.

ILLEGAL QUESTIONS

Job hunters often wonder, how to respond to illegal questions. It is against the law to discriminate against an individual because of age, religion, race, nationality, gender, or skin color. But employers still ask these questions. I believe employers, not really skilled or trained in the art of interviewing, don't recognize that there *are* illegal questions. Some are ignorant and have gotten away with asking these questions in the past. But, illegal questions in an interview is often quite challenging.

Think about this important consideration before you answer an illegal question — "Do you want this job?" Your response should be based on whether or not you want the job. If you take a liberal stand and say, "That's an illegal question and I choose not to answer it," you will probably offend the interviewer. You may make the employer feel ignorant and embarrassed if they indeed didn't know that it was an illegal question. They may disqualify you as a candidate. Job hunters often claim that they feel that the employer is testing them. I find it unlikely, when lawsuits are so prevalent, that an employer would intentionally break the law. Employers who attend my seminar on the hiring interview, state that they don't want to ask illegal questions. My advice to you is this: if you are asked something illegal and you really want the job, simply answer it. Let me give you a couple of examples on handling these tricky questions.

52. "Are you pregnant, and do you have any plans to have children in the near future?"

This was a question I was asked when I interviewed for the Director of Career Center at a community college. It was a panel interview. When the gentleman asked me this question, I was astounded. How could someone interviewing candidates for a state job ask an illegal question like this? I wanted this job, so I said, "At this point in time, my husband and I have no children." It was not necessary for me to elaborate on the question, but I chose to answer it that way because I was interested in the job. Later, I was told by several people that the gentleman was from the "old school" he just didn't realize he was asking an illegal question. Through his naiveté he could have gotten the state into a lot of trouble. I had grounds to sue for gender discrimination. I was not inclined to do so. Incidentally, I did get the job.

53. "What's your husband think about you traveling so much?"

Just answer the question with, "Travel has always been required for other sales positions I've held. I expect it to be a part of this job."

54. "What does your wife think about having to move all the way to Nebraska?"

Be careful. This employer really wants to see if you will truly move to Nebraska and what obstacles your family might impose. Reply with: "Relocating to advance my career is a part of our family goals. Both my wife and I like the Midwest and welcome the chance to move there."

55. "Who's going to care for your kids while you're at work?"

Employers worry about hiring working mothers. Quite often it is because some other woman caused the employer numerous problems due to her family demands. Most employers want reassurance that you will be dependable, productive and pitch in when needed. Be sure to have solid daycare arrangements in place so you can squelch any concerns. I rarely found a case where an employer isn't understanding when something tragic happens to one of your family members once you've been with them for a while. But when they're hiring you, they just want to be sure that you're going to show up. So reassure them that you are a loyal and dedicated employee, and remove any obstacles that they may have in their minds by answering with: "I have a dependable situation that cares for my children even if they are ill. She takes them to appointments, activities, and is flexible so I can work overtime when I am needed."

56. "What country are you from?"

"China. I have been in the US several years and do have a valid green card and working papers to be employed in this country. My experience includes. . ." then reiterate your 60 Second Sell.

57. "The job requires you to work on Sundays. Will this pose a problem with your religion."

"Not at all." Nothing further needs to be said.

58. "How will you adapt to this new job?"

Even though this is not an illegal question, it raises the issue of possible discrimination. Here's an example that shows how a job hunter addressed the unspoken issue of age and dispelled any preconceived ideas the employer might have held about older workers being inflexible or not trainable.

Offer some reasonable proof that your age is an asset. A good response might be: "At Petrich, I always proved to be very flexible and adaptable, frequently taking on new tasks and picking up new skills. I enjoy learning and teaching others. I found that when I deal with difficult customers or solve complex problems I can draw upon my extensive experience and this has repeatedly proved to be an asset in my former positions." You could then go on to describe a specific situation where your experience led you to make the right choice where a less experienced person might have made a mistake. Remember, make the conclusion that with age comes experience and often times wisdom to make better decisions.

If you are lucky you may never be asked to answer an illegal question. If you get one, I suggest you answer the question quickly, and let the interview proceed.

BEHAVIORAL INTERVIEWING

Behavioral Interviewing techniques began gaining some popularity by 1992. This style of interviewing asks you to give very specific examples of positive and negative work situations. The interviewer is trained and well coached on this probing style to determine how you have performed in the past. Then he rates each response to determine and predict your future performance with their company. Expect this style of interviewing to grow. It's often larger, more progressive companies, such as Microsoft and Hewlett Packard that use this style. You're unlikely to know in advance who will use this format, so be prepared. As you can see, these are thought provoking questions. The interviewer will likely take notes on each answer and continue the line of questioning for specifics: specific details, specific illustrations. Practice answering these types of questions by giving concise, detailed examples. Be sure you select examples that clearly sell those skills in the 5 Point Agenda, since that is your predetermined hiring strategy aimed at meeting the needs of that employer. Be concise; tell the whole story in 60 seconds or less. Here are a few questions you might encounter.

59. "Describe a time that you dealt with a stressful work situation."

"I remember a time when we were short staffed over several weeks. I had been working a lot of overtime and so had my staff. One employee called in sick and we had a 5:00 pm deadline that day to finish the newsletter. It would not be possible to extend. I called the three remaining staff in and told them the situation. I asked everyone how we could meet our deadline. They offered good ideas, I had lunch delivered and told everyone that if we finished that day everyone could come in at noon the next day. It was high pressure when everyone was running on low energy, but we did it. I also went to my boss the next day to discuss how we might readjust the workload while we were minus two people." This answer demonstrates teamwork, extra effort and good problem solving skills.

60. "Describe a time when you reprimanded an employee for poor performance."

Show how you gave clear direction and training to enable others to improve at their jobs. "My administrative assistant repeatedly made mistakes in typing correspondence for me. These were errors that probably would have been corrected if she had been proofreading carefully. I sat down with her and brought one letter to her attention, noting all the corrections I had made. I told her very nicely that I was finding too many errors in the letters and asked that she carefully proofread each letter before it was given to me. She said, 'No,' because she felt I wanted them quickly and I always seemed to make changes anyway. I told her that I expected her to proofread each letter and make all corrections before it was given to me. I thought this would save time and that it was very important that our correspondence be perfect before it was mailed out. Since most of the work was highly technical, I suggested she take a class on proofreading and editing. As a result her performance improved."

61. "Describe a time when you felt you made a poor decision."

This is a very tricky question. Try to select an example where your boss admitted to you that she made a mistake too. You might say: "A few years ago, I remember my boss asked me to do a presentation to our board of directors in her absence. I worked on the material, and asked my boss to let me run through the whole thing before the meeting. On the morning I was to do that, my boss got tied up so I never got her input on my research and data. I decided to just do the handouts and was embarrassed at the meeting when my figures and marketing data were heavily questioned. I got intimidated and nervous and stumbled through their questions. I made a poor choice when I did not get any other input when my boss was unable to assist me. She did apologize to me later and took some of the responsibility for not making the time to help me before the meeting. I learned a valuable lesson about teamwork that day, one that has helped me become a better supervisor."

62. "Describe the environment that motivates your productivity."

This question often has you reveal some important clues on your true work style. You might answer with: "I find that I am most productive in an organization that expects me to do a good job, rewards me well, and has the needed resources to accomplish the goals. If you check with my references you'll find that I am a self-starter, happy when there are volumes of work to complete, and that I can be counted on to get it done right and on time." You might then ask them "How much autonomy will I have in this job?" Then you can learn how this job might suit your needs. Be sure to comment on any specifics that they reply with.

FIRINGS/LAYOFFS/ WORK GAPS/REENTRY

63. "Were you fired from your last job or why did you leave your last job?"

People who have been fired or laid off are very fearful that no one's going to hire them again. In this day and age, the average employee will have 10.3 job changes and with downsizing and corporate layoffs happening all over the place, you're likely to find yourself in this situation once or twice. Actually, the fear and concern that you feel is probably stronger inside you than it is with the actual employer. In most instances, the fact that you were fired is not going to stop you from being hired again. But if you believe it's going to be held against you, then you can create a lot of doubt in the employer's mind just by the way you answer the question.

To prepare an answer, there are a couple of techniques that I'd suggest. First, if you were fired because of a personal conflict with another person at your former position, recognize that almost 80% of all firings are the result of interpersonal conflict on the job. Incompetent workers keep their jobs, but people with personality conflicts usually, somewhere along the line, lose theirs. So if you've been fired, for whatever reason, take pen and paper and then write out some sample answers. Analyze what took place and why were you let go. Let's say you couldn't get along with your supervisor. You had differences of opinion, and because of those differences of opinion, the supervisor eventually made the decision to fire you. Here's how to answer this very difficult question.

"One of the most important things that I've learned since I left my last job is the importance of having open communication. My boss was not a person that talked about goals or expectations, but instead reacted when something went wrong. I'm the type of person who likes to get feedback so that I know if I'm doing a good job, if I'm meeting expectations, or if something's going haywire, I can work on correcting it. There was a problem with the budget process at my last job. I thought we had more time to retrieve the information than we did. The information from other areas needed to be analyzed and we had no control to speed up getting the other departments to respond faster. I created a conflict with my boss by trying to get him to go to the departments and get the information sent to us faster and in a different form. My boss felt differently than I and decided that because of the conflict between us that he should let me go. I've learned a lot since then, and I know that it's going to be very important in my new job to make sure that I find a supervisor that has the open communication that I work well with. If you call my former employer, he would tell you that I was a good worker, that I brought strong financial and accounting skills to the workplace, even my supervisory ability with my other staff worked well. These strengths were never in question." As you can see, this is an answer that is well thought out. The candidate planned how to answer the question. Point out where there was a problem, and where there wasn't, so the employer gets a feeling that yes, maybe you just didn't get along with that supervisor because of poor communication and the need for stronger leadership.

If you were laid off, you might respond: "My company, like so many others, has restructured and my position was eliminated during the reorganization." or "My company decided to close its regional office and my entire department was let go." In either answer end with "That's why I am presently available." Be careful with this answer so that your voice and tone doesn't express desperation. It is important to not appear to want any job, but to be seeking the right opportunity. You may feel desperate, but practice *not* letting that feeling sneak into your tone. The employer wants to believe you really want *their* job, not just any job.

64. I've noticed there was a period of time when you weren't employed. Tell me about it.

Examine your reason for the work gap. The most frequent reasons are time between employment, a personal illness, a family illness, failed self-employment, maternity, or raising young children. The importance here is to construct your answer to show that whatever the problem was, it has been resolved and your performance, attendance, and motivation will all be top notch now. To explain children or maternity and just returning, try "I took time off to have a child (children). I have been able to secure excellent daycare that will ensure that I'll be able to work everyday and be a productive employee." Be willing to answer any follow-up questions that the employer might ask, such as: "What will you do when the child is sick? Occasionally we need this person to work overtime, will that be a problem? What are the hours that the daycare is open? How have you prepared to handle the pressures of this position and the demands of a new family member? The employer's concerns center around: 1) How productive will you be? 2) Will your mind be on your work? 3) Will you be reliable? 4) What ways will your situation impact your ability to do the job — no overtime, changing hours, or absenteeism. Your most important goal is to learn whether or not this employer's situation will work for you. The employer expects you to show up, on time, and complete your assigned workload. Employers often get leery about hiring mothers because they have often had bad experiences in the past. I hired an assistant who insisted that she'd never missed a day of work while she was pregnant or when she returned. Once hired, she immediately began to experience problems — daycare for two children was very high; she wanted to change hours to fit her schedule and reduce her daycare costs. Unfortunately, this was at the expense of closing the office, so she could come in late. She only lasted two months and once let go, my boss vowed never to hire a mother again. Many employers have had a bad experience like I did. Therefore, when you are returning to work after maternity breaks, arrange daycare that will care for mildly sick children (flu, colds) or establish a secondary system (family, friend, neighbor) who will care for the child if the care center doesn't. Be sure that you have plenty of leeway to drop off and pick up your children. That way, if you need to work a little overtime, you will be able to. Don't expect or ask employers to change the position's hours to fit your daycare schedule. If you can't work their hours, then drop out of consideration for that job. It is best to be honest. Predetermine your necessary take home salary by subtracting taxes and daycare costs. This allows you a guideline to judge potential jobs realistically.

When answering any work-gap questions dealing with unemployment, simply say "I was seeking a new position at that time." Be prepared for a question on why you left the job prior to the unemployed period. Always reassure the employer about your current reliability and on-the-job productivity.

65. You've been unemployed quite awhile, why haven't you obtained a job before this?

Most job hunters underestimate the length of time the job search process requires, so they take extended vacations or regroup because they are too drained by the layoff or firing. It's important to note that the average job search takes four to six months. If you've been unemployed for more than one year, you need a very good reason. An appropriate response might be: "I did take some time to really evaluate my career and focus the direction of my search. I've been actively job hunting several months and am meeting with employers to find a position that will utilize my skills and allow me to be a contributing part of their team."

If the unemployment was due to a personal problem or illness, you could explain with: "A personal crisis arose in my family that required my time and energy. It was difficult emotionally and so I left my position because my focus could not be on my job. Now the situation is completely resolved. I am ready and eager to work. I feel that my previous strengths of. . .(mention two or three of your most marketable abilities) will assist me in again being an asset to my employer." Sometimes you can mention the incident — illness, divorce, death, accident — but use your judgment. No employer will believe you've completely recovered from the death of your spouse in four weeks. I believe it is best not to give many details and try to move on quickly and avoid a lengthy discussion of this issue.

66. "Can we check with your current employer?"

This question often makes job hunters very nervous when their employer doesn't know they are looking for a job. To say no, try this "My current employer is not aware I am looking for a new position and contacting him could jeopardize the job I have. I have the names of three references here who are very familiar with my work that you can call." If you can show copies of past performance appraisals (only excellent ones) do so at this time.

In large companies you may have someone who can be a reference besides your immediate boss, so try this approach: "My immediate boss is unaware that I am looking for a more challenging position and I'd prefer he not be called. I do work with the operations manager daily as part of my duties and you could contact her. I've put her name and number first on my reference list. The other two people have worked with me in the past in supervisory roles. I am sure they can answer any questions you have."

67. "Describe your management style in dealing with staff and coworkers."

The more you know about the employer, the easier it will be to frame your answer to demonstrate your competent leadership capabilities. Your research should direct how you answer this question. Some positions require a firm approach, some decisive decision making, other companies like the micro manager approach, still others prefer an open approachable style. Dictatorial styles are very passé, but some old fashioned employers might expect that from their managers. Analyze your style and that of the company, then create your answer. You could say "I expect myself and my staff to do our jobs well. I do my best to ensure they have the resources and the necessary training to be top performers. I hold each person accountable for doing their job and enforce company policies. I'm a reasonable person. I'll listen to the coworker's, staff, or client's needs and will change policies that become outdated or ineffective. I have found that encouraging open communications, listening to my staff's ideas and being fair in my decisions has worked well in building a productive team in the past."

68. "What would you find difficult from what you understand about this job?"

The interviewer is looking for you to expound upon some area or weakness you have. Perhaps you've heard something that makes *you* wonder about your performance ability. In that case, ask a question such as "I need to know more about how you use your computer systems and how the software is used in the job." Or "Could you tell me more about how large your budget is, the resources and staff available assigned to this project first?" Quantify their needs, their situation, and then answer. When citing a potential problem, explain that you learn quickly and that whatever appears to be a problem will be easily solved.

If this job seems to be in line with your abilities, just start with "I don't see any difficulties and feel I'll quickly adjust. . ." then continue with your 60 Second Sell.

69. "What makes you qualified?"

Using your 60 Second Sell will serve you best in responding to this one.

70. "How do you handle stress?"

Most jobs have some stress or pressure involved and this question asks how you would respond to that stress. Be forewarned that if you bring up a specific stressful situation at work you will be asked all the details of why it happened, who contributed, what you did and didn't do, plus possibly raise doubts about your effectiveness to handle the work without creating stressful environments for yourself and others. Be sure to prepare for these in advance to prevent getting into hot water with a poor example. A good response can say "Often times stress results from inadequate time management and then feeling panicked at the end to get the job done and meet a deadline. I try to plan ahead and work efficiently to avoid last minute pressure cooker situations. There are times though when unforeseen circumstances create a stressful situation. Whenever that happens to me, I draw on my previous experience, examine what have I done in the past that has worked to help me decide how to effectively handle this present situation. The fact that I exercise three or four times a week also helps. I find it reduces my stress and increases my energy and ability to think clearly and perform better at my job."

TECHNICAL EXPERTISE
AND SPECIALTY QUESTIONS

It is a reasonable assumption that you will be asked very specific questions related to your field. Once you've gained experience in an industry and job area, you'll need to be able to give examples and answer related questions. A computer programmer should expect numerous questions concerning the languages she knows, the types of software and application she worked on. Likewise, a trainer might be asked questions about the subject, teaching style, curriculum development, and learning patterns.

Write up five to ten questions you think you might get asked concerning your field. Then practice answering them. Again, remember the guidelines — short, concise answers of less than 60 seconds, using real work examples to demonstrate how you've done this work before.

10 QUESTIONS FOR COLLEGE
STUDENTS AND NEW GRADS

Most students have little or no related work experience when they go to the interview for their first professional job. You wonder what you should say, how you should answer those questions. You often are very nervous.

Preparation can help relieve some of that anxiety and allow you to effectively communicate the skills you do have. Most often, you've had a "McJob" — working in a fast food restaurant. You learned customer service skills and how to work under pressure. Dependability became a personal habit. Be sure to examine all work experience and activities for evidence of leadership or business skills, organizational abilities, time management skills, research, analysis, or report writing abilities. Develop your 5 Point Agenda and 60 Second Sell after you have researched and learned the job duties and skills necessary to do the employer's entry level job.

Practice answering questions with full and complete responses that get your point across in 60 seconds or less. Here are ten frequently asked questions you should be able to effectively answer.

1. "What are your long-range and short-range goals and objectives? How are you preparing yourself to achieve them?"

The interviewer wants to see how focused you are and how realistic. The interviewer wonders about the training time that you'll need to become productive and how long you'll stay once they have invested time training you. A good response might be a very honest one. "My short term goal is to get a job that will provide me with the training and environment to use the skills I've developed in college. I'm a very hard worker and a quick learner so I want an environment where I can contribute. I believe that once I'm working, I'll be exposed to many areas of business that I haven't seen yet, so I plan to keep my long term options open while I explore numerous possibilities." This response doesn't jeopardize your chances for a position by mapping out a career agenda such as "next year I'm off to law school" that doesn't fit into the employer's plans. Show flexibility, adaptability and definitely a realistic attitude about your future opportunities.

2. "Describe your ideal job and location."

Tricky question, as you often don't know what your *ideal* job is and often say you'll move anywhere. Most students will move to get a job. Analyze where you will and won't move. Then respond with "I really am willing to move wherever the company needs me, though I'm concentrating my search on the East Coast. My ideal job is an environment that allows me to learn, gain new skills, and be a productive worker. It is also very important for me to know that I'm helping people through my efforts." Or to end with "It's important that I make a contribution to the company."

3. "What two or three accomplishments have given you the most satisfaction? Why?"

Here is a great opportunity to stress two or three points in your 5 Point Agenda. Let's say organizational skills are one point and time management is another. You could respond "Graduating from college is a big accomplishment for me and so was getting that A in statistics. In both cases, I held a part time job while attending school. I often needed to prioritize and plan out my schedule, setting aside the time to study and do papers. Statistics was a challenging course for me and required a lot of extra effort. I organized a study group and I worked on problems every day. I felt pressured by the job, but needed to work to cover tuition costs, so I cut out extra socializing for a few weeks and pulled an A. I felt like my hard work paid off in both cases and that's been really satisfying."

4.   "What led you to choose your field or major of study?"

"Liberal Arts has taught me to think out problems, research and analyze data and develop good written communication skills. I've found Sociology to be interesting with it's broad based analysis of society's behavior patterns. My classes required eight to nine books per course so I feel I've also developed excellent time management skills when tackling a heavy workload." Another approach is to show how your major is a building block. If you were an accounting major, your answer might be very specific, such as "I started out in the business track and took Fundamentals of Accounting my freshman year. I loved it. I loved the analytical challenge and I've always had a strong ability when working with numbers. I decided to be an accountant after that class and am a student member of the state CPA society. It's a field I know I will succeed in, as I've done very well in my college program."

5.   "What college subjects did you like best? Least? Why?"

This tells the interviewer your strengths and your weaknesses and therein lies the tricky questions. Your answer must illustrate interest in areas necessary to do their job, and denote only subjects that are unrelated, that you disliked. You could create an answer like this, substituting your favorite subject, "Psychology classes were my favorites and my major. I loved learning about human behavior, interaction and helping others deal with behavior difficulties. I least liked the modern art class. I found it too abstract for me."

6.   "Do you have plans for continued study? An advanced degree?"

Tricky question here. The interviewer is trying another avenue to access your goals and how it will fit into his organization's needs. If you do not plan to go on, simply say "At this time, I plan to land a position and work hard to be productive. I don't have any current plans to go on." If you are planning further education you could say, "I plan to get two or three years of engineering work first, and then I think I'd like to enroll in an evening MBA program. I know that it's very demanding to handle both a full time job and coursework, but I think I can, as I worked all through college. I do feel it is important now to move from the classroom to a manufacturing setting because there's a lot to learn on the job before I pursue more education."

7. "In what part-time or summer jobs have you been most interested? Why?"

Most part time jobs are not interesting and you often worked for the money. Try to answer the question by noting something you did like, for example "I lived in a small town and was very lucky to get any job. I worked as a receptionist for a real estate office. I enjoyed talking to people who called especially when I could answer their questions or solve their problem. The best part of my job was a small two week project I worked on. Their secretary got sick and I did a large spreadsheet project for them. My boss was thrilled I could enter data and that I knew EXCEL. I spent extra hours on my own time, learning the program so I could make the tables easy for everyone to use. I really enjoyed that and want a position that requires a lot of computer work."

8. "What have you learned from the jobs you've had?"

The answer is your 60 Second Sell as it relates to jobs and not course work. Or you could say "I've learned how important it is to be on time, to be at work every day and to work hard while I'm there. When I was a waitress, it really made it hard on everyone if another waitress called in sick. One night I had all the tables because both waitresses were sick. It was a very high pressure, intense night. I worked hard and fast, but was tremendously overloaded. Anyone else would have quit. But, I knew that the employer was counting on me so I worked that night alone. I also learned that it's crucial to make every effort to be at the job *every* day."

9. "If you were on an eight hour transatlantic flight, who would you want to sit next to you and what would you talk about?"

The interviewer is interested in having you reveal more of your personality, your depth, and personal interests. Resist saying the current movie star heart throb or model because he or she is so gorgeous. Better to illustrate depth and think before you answer. Select someone that could teach you something. A notable business person or political figure are good choices. A business student could say, "Bill Gates. I'm fascinated by Microsoft's products and the company as a whole. I think he's a true visionary. I would spend the time learning about the roles he thinks computers will play in the future, the information technology changes he foresees and how that will impact our whole society, and the way we conduct business."

10. "How do you think a friend or professor who knows you well would describe you?"

Sell yourself through your friend or professor's eyes by saying, "They would tell you. . ." then go into your 60 Second Sell. Adding that you're a conscientious, hard worker is always a plus too.

DO YOUR BEST

Preparing for potential questions in advance will give you a big advantage over the numerous job hunters who do not prepare. When you write out answers, you need to analyze the difficult ones and calmly select effective answers that demonstrate to the employer that you can and will do their job. Actually, why people think questions are so tough or so difficult is because they haven't really thought about them. They got stumped because they had no plan to follow, no previous ideas jotted down. Short, concise answers of less than 60 seconds that avoid the mine fields can result in *you* landing the job. Your interview is really where the employer decides whether or not to hire you. Work hard to do your best. You will not win every time, but you'll improve with each interview and get better at effectively marketing your abilities. Always remember our mantra — 60 Seconds and You're Hired.

5

QUESTIONS YOU SHOULD ASK

At some point in every interview the employer will ask "Do you have any questions?" Often times the candidate searches to ask anything, because they had not prepared their own list of questions in advance. This will not happen to you. Take the time before the interview to think about what information you need to aid you in deciding if this is a good position and fit for you. This is a very important part of the interviewing process. The employer often puts a lot of weight on what you ask. People have a hard time "thinking up" their questions. The best questions that you want to ask are strictly job-related and duty-related. You can ask all about the company's benefits, sick leave, pension programs, *after* you've gotten the job offer.

HOW TO IMPRESS THE EMPLOYER

Before the interview, prepare a list of pertinent questions that you want answered to determine if this position is really a good fit for you. Write or type out your questions on a piece of paper that you can take out when it's your turn to ask questions. The employer is impressed that you cared enough about their position to think through their needs, their duties. Do not bring up any questions about salary or benefits at this time. Focus on determining if you want to do their job. Your questions also give insight into your thoroughness when given important responsibilities. Ten to fifteen questions are a reasonable number to have on your list. Many will have been answered during the interview. Bring up anything the employer mentioned you want to know more about. If by chance they have already answered all your questions, you could say something like this "As I check over my list, my questions on your software were covered as well as the equipment you use. We discussed budgets and training policies. I guess you've covered everything already."

25 QUESTIONS YOU COULD ASK

Here are 25 questions that you can consider asking. Notice how each one is designed to gather details on doing the job and learning more about the organization's work culture and environment.

- What are the day-to-day responsibilities that I'll have in this job?

- Who will I be supervising?

- Could you explain your organizational structure to me?

- What is the organization's plan for the next five years, and how does this department or division fit in?

- Will we be expanding, bringing on any new products or new services that I should be aware of?

- Could you describe to me your typical management style and the type of employee that works well with you?

- What are some of the skills and abilities you see as necessary for someone to succeed in this job?

- What challenges might I encounter if I take on this position?

- What are your major concerns that need to be immediately addressed in this job?

- What areas in this job would you like improved?

- What is your company's policy on providing seminars, workshops, and training so the employees can keep up on their skills or acquire new skills?

- What is the budget this department operates with?

- Are there any restraints or cutbacks planned that would decrease those budgets?

- What particular computer equipment and software do you use here?

- Are any new equipment purchases planned?

- What personality traits do you think are necessary to succeed in this job?

- Will I be working as a team or alone?

- What committees will I participate in?

- How will my leadership responsibilities and performance be measured? By whom?

- To what extent are the functions of this department considered important by upper management?

- Are there any weaknesses in the department that you are working on improving?

- What are the company's two year goals, long term goals?

- What are the department's goals and how do they fit into the company's mission?

- What are the company's strengths and weaknesses compared to its competition?

X ▪ How does the reporting structure work here? What are acceptable channels of communication?

X ▪ What new endeavors is the company currently undertaking?

6

SALARY QUESTIONS

The hardest questions can be those that deal with salary. Handling them like a pro can assure you of obtaining the highest offer possible from an employer.

SALARY HISTORY

Want ads frequently request salary history. Applications commonly ask for previous salary information. Why? To screen applicants OUT. This screening tool has nothing to do with your exceptional abilities to do the job — only the dollar and cents cost. The best strategy to deal with this is to simply send nothing. Leave any salary requests blank. Employers have been known to increase the salary, change the job title, add more benefits, paying thousands more than they initially set forth in order to hire the person that they *wanted* for the job. Job hunters eliminate themselves from consideration not only when their salary history is high, but also if it appears to be too low. The employer concludes that the candidate is not as good as the resume says or he would be making more money. Always, always, always — establish your value first. Here's why.

SECRETS OF ESTABLISHING YOUR VALUE

People want what they want. Employers too. That's the psychology that becomes your competitive edge in the salary negotiations process when you are the one they want. Once the employer feels they must have *you* to do the work there is a role reversal. Now they need to recruit and sell you on taking their job. It all begins with knowing what your skills and abilities are worth, then communicating that value to an employer. The end result is they *must* have you to do the job.

HOW TO LEARN WHAT THEY WILL PAY

To accurately assess your value in the workplace, I suggest that you conduct an investigation into what comparable jobs pay for the job title you are looking for in your geographical area. There are several places to find this information. Associations, and business magazines frequently publish annual salary surveys. They often break down salary by job title, level of experience, and by geographical regions. The Department of Labor publishes numerous salary lists. Your best bet is to ask the reference librarian to help you find the salary information you seek. Lastly, consider asking colleagues this question: "I'm seeking a new position as an Electrical Engineer for a manufacturing company. I have five years experience. If I ask for a salary of $35,000, do you think that is reasonable? Would it be reasonable for your company?" Another technique is to ask "What is the typical range this job would pay in your company?" Gather the facts early so you can have a reasonable expectation of the salary you could ask and be given.

ANSWERING THE QUESTION

"What salary do you expect if we offer you the job?" Too often, job hunters just throw out a number. That is a critical mistake. Always remember that the first person who mentions money loses. Loses in terms of real dollars. And, in your case, sometimes loses the job. If we use the psychology of people wanting what they want, we must first make them want us. So, try these answers "I expect to be fairly compensated for my work. I feel confident that if we determine I'm the right person to do the job, we can reach an agreement. To me, it's the job itself that is most important." This approach can often detour the employer to move on.

A more persistent interviewer may say "Well, we need to determine salary expectations. What figure do you expect?" Answer with "What is the salary range that this position pays?" This volleyball technique encourages them to give you the figure. Typically they will say "$35,000 — $40,000." You respond "I'm within your range," or if it is low "I'm near that range" and then go on with the interview. Try to avoid lengthy salary discussions. At this stage in the interview, mention a figure too low (you certainly must lack the skills to do their job) or too high (you'd never work for less) and the interviewer will determine you are not the one they want, based on these answers alone.

Your winning strategy is this — keep the conversation centered on how well you can do their job. Continually sell your 5 Point Agenda itinerary. Utilize your 60 Second Sell whenever appropriate. These will market your best strengths and influence the employer to decide he *must* have you. Once the job offer has been formally made, THEN it's the right time to discuss and negotiate the salary you want and deserve for performing that job.

7

NEGOTIATING THE BEST DEAL

As the employer says "You got the job," you mumble some pleasantry as you silently scream YES! If you intend to negotiate for any benefits or salary increase, then as tempting as it is to just accept, I advise you to refrain from that outburst and say "I'd like to meet with you tomorrow and discuss your offer and all the details." If they haven't stated the salary, ask it. Arrange the meeting time. If you are on the phone, end the conversation. If you are face to face, try to reset for the next day if possible. You have a lot of preparation to do, especially if you want the employer to raise the offer. This meeting you just arranged is called the Negotiations Interview and there is a formula to follow to successfully negotiate a better compensation package.

DETERMINE THE RISKS

Salary negotiations is a game — a sophisticated game — but a game nonetheless. To be successful, you must enter this playing arena fully equipped with knowledge and appropriate negotiation strategies.

Your first step is to assess the employer's compensation system and degree of flexibility. Most employers operate within the following systems:

- **Fixed Offer** — Some employers simply do not negotiate. They offer a take-it-or-leave-it deal.

- **Pay Grade System** — A predetermined range is set for the job, based on duties required. Where you fall in this range is determined by your years of experience. This system rarely offers the top salary to anyone, it is earned in raises over the years. To significantly raise the salary, the employer often has to reclassify the job in a higher pay grade. This has been known to happen especially when it has been established that the employer underestimated the skills necessary to adequately perform the job.

- **Negotiable Guidelines** — This is the best situation. The employer has more liberty to raise or lower the salary as he sees fit. This allows you the best chance to bargain for your services.

Your next step is to assess the job market's supply of qualified candidates. If there were others who are equally qualified and the employer would be happy with any of them — this is a clue that your negotiating power is reduced. Then again, I've seen clients sail through resume stacks of 400 potential employees right to the top, succeed after nine hours of interviewing and be offered the job. The employer really wanted them and so they were able to secure excellent compensation packages in spite of the competition. They argued that they were the best of the lot. The employer agreed and paid dearly to have them join their team.

The final step before you begin the face-to-face negotiations is to determine what is a fair offer — particularly if you've been overpaid or underpaid. During your salary survey, you should have determined what was a fair expectation. When leaving a large Fortune 500 company for a smaller organization, the offers are usually less. Likewise, moving from an underpaid situation, how much more is enough? Small employers often offer less salary, fewer benefits in exchange for more responsibility and interesting, challenging jobs. Cautiously determine the employer's compensation style. *Asking* for more compensation properly rarely risks an offer being withdrawn, but *demanding* more can. Investigate and use the Negotiations Strategies. Predetermine a *fair, reasonable* goal for both you and the employer.

NEGOTIATION STRATEGIES

When you arrive at the negotiation interview, implement these techniques in your efforts to get the best deal.

1. **Confident Approach**. Your tone often affects the results of this whole process. Exude enthusiasm for the job. Reconfirm your ability to do the job. Have a win/win attitude. To begin the conversation, ask about the benefits, vacations, overtime. Grill them on all these terms. Ask for what is policy and what is practiced. Often times the policy is that you receive compensation time for your overtime hours. The practice may be that you are absolutely discouraged from ever using it. Learn the rules and practices.

   To lead into the discussion about salary, say "I'm really interested in the position. I was a little disappointed with the offer being lower than I expected." Then be quiet and remain quiet while the employer makes the next move. Another approach is "I'm very interested in the job, is there a possibility of negotiating on the salary here?" Smile and follow the employer's lead.

2. **Negotiate to Get the Money Up Front**. Bonuses, raises all have a way of never happening down the line. Every dollar you negotiate into the salary base now is more money you can spend on things you and your family want. Work towards the extra money up front. The negotiations could give you in one hour what would take years to acquire with raises.

3. **Try**. Most people are afraid to try. Especially women and the unemployed person. Women by nature devalue themselves. They don't recognize their complete worth in the workplace and rarely demand it. Salary studies still reveal women are paid substantially lower than men. I encourage women to expect and seek comparable compensation for the job performed.

   The unemployed person sits in a difficult spot. They often need the job and the employer knows it. In this situation, reiterate what you bring and try to get fair compensation. Often times the employer will give a low ball offer just to see

if you would take it. Test the waters to see if there is room for
them to pay more.

4. **Settle for the Middle**. Negotiations often end with both
    sides compromising. Allow room to do just that. If the
    employer offers $52,000 and you want $55,000 — try this.
    "We're pretty close in terms of salary. I was thinking with my
    ten years of experience that $57,000 is more in line." Be
    willing to give a little — you'll still be $3,000 ahead when
    you settle for $55,000.

5. **Money and What Else?** Compensation benefits come in
    very complex packages from nothing at all to free day care
    services. Evaluate the extra value a company's medical plan
    adds. What about vacation time, flexible hours, tuition
    reimbursement, fewer hours, days off, relocation expenses,
    cars, expense accounts, bonuses? Perhaps the salary cannot
    be raised, but additional benefits could be added. Look
    closely at the medical plan. What kind of coverage is
    provided? What deductibles does the plan include? Who pays
    for dependents? If you pay, what will that cost be? My clients
    have successfully argued for a higher salary to compensate
    for switching medical plans where the old employer covered
    the entire family and the new one covers just the employee.
    Predetermine what is important to you.

    Vacations and days off can often be negotiated. Be careful
    because other staff often resent favoritism to a new
    employee. And just because you had four weeks vacation
    from your last boss (with ten years of service), it is unlikely
    the new company will give you four weeks. Be flexible, but
    be reasonable.

6. **Focus on the Employer's Needs**. Resell yourself throughout
    this process. Reaffirm the reasons they want you, how you
    will solve their problems. Mention your 60 Second Sell and
    stress how quickly you will be productive. In other words,
    give them reasons to pay you more. Create a chart (I call it
    the Hiring Chart) that outlines the job "needs" and your
    abilities to do the job, your "contributions." See a sample
    Hiring Chart on page 55.

Patty Promotions
Director of Promotions

NEEDS	CONTRIBUTIONS
Creative	12 years in creative services.
Promotions	Promotion/advertising for #1 independent TV station in L.A. using direct mail, publicity campaign, sales presentation, and special events.
Writing	Press releases, bios, on-air promotion, business proposals.
Public Relations	Extensive experience working with print, broadcast, media, celebrities, agencies.
Budgets	Budgets/advertising for TV station in L.A. emphasizing cost effective spending.
Events	Coordinator for Sammy Davis Jr.'s 60th birthday video, coordinated special gallery exhibitions, organizing celebrity appearances.
Supervision	Trained staff. Easily coordinate others into a cohesive team.
Client/Customer Relations	Developed new business. Built solid, long lasting client relationships.
Sponsorship	Excellent research skills to develop prospect list for joint sponsorship and events to maximize visibility.
Sales	Able to prospect, evaluate leads, write proposals, and close sales effectively.

Give the employer your Hiring Chart to go over *their* needs and detail your contributions. Let the employer keep this chart. It's proof of why he should pay you more money. It may be helpful if he needs to go to his boss to ask for your additional salary.

7. **Know Your Bottom Line**. Only you can decide when the offer is too low, too much compromise. Never ever bluff. Offers can be withdrawn when a job hunter says "$51,000 is as low as I will accept." Be prepared to keep looking. Sometimes that is the right move for you. Decide what is the lowest you can reasonably accept to cover your bills and concentrate on succeeding in the job and not immediately looking for another higher paying one.

8. **Practice**. Think through the negotiation interview. Visualize a successful outcome. Then, ask a friend to role play the interview. Defend why you are worth the money. Listen to the feedback — did you convince them? This preparation will decrease your anxiety and increase your confidence.

9. **Employment Letter**. Once you have agreed upon all the terms, ask for an employment letter. You can offer to write it or the employer can, but be sure the employer signs it. This letter should outline all the terms of your employment. Cover salary, starting date, benefits, particularly note anything different from the organization's normal policies. Too many promises are made and quickly forgotten once you start the job. Get the details in writing so there are no misunderstandings later.

10. **Multiple Offers**. Oh, the luxury of choices. Be **sure** there is another choice. Once a firm offer is made, job hunters often become convinced that the employer wants them for the other job for which they just interviewed as well. Do they? Employers don't like to be pushed because you have "other opportunities." A straight forward approach works best. Call the other employers with whom you interviewed and tell them you have a firm offer. Ask them for a status report. Tell them your time line and wait. If they are going to make you a firm offer, they will within that time limit. Sometimes you

are not their first choice and they will say so. Either way, you will know where you stand. A job in hand is a real job — not a hope, dream, or belief. Decide with facts, not gut instinct.

When two solid offers stand, decide which one you want and then negotiate harder for the best terms they can offer.

Your four keys to success start with first asking for a fair price, second continuously selling yourself and reiterating your worth, third remembering that whoever mentions money first loses, and finally evaluating your long term goals and the career growth or security this opportunity offers.

8

TEN TYPES OF
INTERVIEWS

When the employer calls to say "We'd like you to come in for an interview," it's important to respond with two questions. First, ask "Certainly, may I ask what dates and times you have available?" You are probing to determine how many people they are talking to. Try to be the last person on any given day. When you are sandwiched between others, the interviews often get hurried, with less time for important notes in between. Plus the interviewer gets bored. At the end of a day, you must show enthusiasm and smile warmly using the 60 Second Sell quickly to develop rapport and interest to leave the employer with a lasting impression.

The second question to ask is about the type of interview. Try to gather as much information as possible. Ask "Whom will I be interviewing with?" Note their name and title. Probe to see if the person will share more information about the job duties. Ask if a complete job description is available. If yes, have that faxed to your nearest local fax machine to aid you in your preparation. Be sure to get clear directions to their office.

Here are some insights to aid you in dealing with the various types of interviews you might encounter.

SCREENING

This initial interview is designed to narrow the pool of acceptable candidates and determine whom to call in for a full interview. Face-to-face this is often done with a human resource person or company recruiter; almost always on a one to one basis. The second way is via telephone, most often on a one-on-one basis also. One client faced a conference call with three board members on the line, so that can happen, but it's less common.

Let's discuss a telephone interview first. The interviewer knows they will catch you off guard. They often call in the evenings or on weekends. I've personally conducted a lot of these for employers and I'm amazed at how many people say it is OK to talk when there are obviously TV, loud children, and distracting events going on. Preparation is the key to success and this screening is the first hurdle along the way. When you get this call, tell the person you are just finishing something and can you call them back in ten minutes. Then prepare yourself. Find a quiet spot, get your resume out and think about the questions they will ask. The employer's objective is to clarify experience and salary expectations. Mentally rehearse your answers. Have a pen and paper in front of you. Jot down their name and take notes as they ask you a question. Smile, so your voice sounds friendly. They need to hear that you have the experience to do their job. Demonstrate that you do with answers that are less than 60 seconds, but more than "yes" or "no."

The face-to-face screening interview seeks to weed out the unqualified and overpriced. The disadvantage here is that the human resource person often is not specifically familiar with all the details of the job. They are generalists and seek to validate job experience, not job potential. Be sure to structure answers to demonstrate how you have done the work in the past. Your 60 Second Sell will be effective in outlining your strengths. These interviews usually last 20 minutes. To move to the next level you must convince this person that you *can* do the job. Prepare accordingly.

HIRING

This is a face-to-face, one-on-one interview. This format allows you to build rapport and establish a base to judge your potential boss, who is most often the person conducting the interview. The person may be a well trained interviewer. These are found most often in large progressive companies like Microsoft or Hewlett Packard. Often, the person has no formal interview training and they may ask irrelevant questions or talk too long. Always help them by offering leading information. A client interviewed with a manager who spent 20 minutes talking about the job. She took notes. She asked questions and then used the information to vary one aspect of her 60 Second Sell. Another client exclaimed that it seemed that the interviewer would never let her speak. After 30 minutes, she offered this comment, shaking her head in agreement, "I understand why customer service skills are so important to you. In my last position, I rewrote our customer service policy. My research supported the facts that our clients were dissatisfied with busy phone lines and untrained staff. I implemented a new system that more quickly answered calls. Then I developed a training program with manual and practice telephone sessions. We saw a vast improvement over this last year. What do you feel needs to be done here?" If nothing else, this person took control, but showed the employer she heard his concern, understood, and could solve his problems. It is necessary to try to direct the questioning to your strengths where you can demonstrate solutions.

All one-on-one interviews require a firm handshake, smile, eye contact, and rapport building demeanor — open and self-confident, sending the message that you can solve their problems.

SECOND

This is usually either with the same person or someone else in upper management, usually the first interviewer's boss.

You have gathered information at the first interview and should be clear about the employer's true needs. Often, only two or three top candidates remain as possibilities for this job. Prepare and adjust your 60 Second Sell with answers to address their true needs. Refer whenever possible to something the interviewer noted in the first meeting. Show enthusiasm and give examples. This employer wants to get to know you better. They want to learn about you, your personality, and determine if they still like you. They want to confirm whether you are the best fit available. Work to assure them with examples and work samples. Demonstrate an understanding for their needs and how you can offer solutions.

The boss's boss, looks more globally. How do you fit into the big picture? Will you be promotion material? Others worry that you will want a promotion too soon and they want someone to stay and do the job they are trying to hire for. You must show your ability to meet company goals, be productive, and easy to work with. You absolutely must convince this person you can do the job and are very willing to do it.

Show enthusiasm for the position and pride in your past accomplishments. Ask questions about the company's future and how the job and the division fits into the company's short and long term goals.

MULTIPLE

Key positions — CEOs, VPs, Presidents, CFOs, Sales Managers, Human Resource Managers, Public Relation Directors, Marketing and Advertising Directors — often go through a lengthy multi-meeting process. You will most likely meet several key administrators with the process taking six to ten hours. Companies feel that this extensive courtship time allows them to uncover your true weaknesses and determine whether or not they can live with those failings. A challenge in this process is that each person often has a slightly different agenda. Try to analyze each person by job title and predetermine their concerns. Think about how your role would interact with them and prepare answers and your 60 Second Sell accordingly. Many companies have you meet with your potential staff. They put a lot of weight into the staff comments — be open and friendly with any staff. Clearly explain what you are like as a manager and learn what they like. Stress that you treat everyone fairly. Watch workplace situation questions — they often are a red flag that there is a staff conflict. Try not to deal with them in the interview; just reiterate you treat people fairly. Often, political situations with two conflicting staff must be learned about later during the negotiation interview, gaining direction from top management on their expectations of how that problem should be dealt with.

PANEL

This is often challenging because it is difficult to determine who has the ultimate decision making power and it is intimidating facing several people with varying agendas and questions. Topics easily switch from one question to the next, eliminating the flow and rapport that is easier to create when you're speaking to only one person.

If possible, try to determine who has the final decision making power and always address that person's needs and concerns in the overall spectrum. Create your answers and your 60 Second Sell as if you were speaking directly to this person.

There will be times where it is unknown who is the true decision maker. Address the needs as a group, but focus your answers in relation to your boss and her boss's needs.

When you enter the room, if possible shake hands firmly and smile as you are introduced to each person. Mention their name. If a table separates you, nod and greet each person by name. "Hello Tom," "Nice to meet you Mary," "Bob." Address the answer to the person who asks the question. Be sure to answer the question. Qualify the question if you want more information before you answer. Look directly at the person as you respond. Only sweep the others if you are experienced at this technique for they may be writing and make you nervous thinking they aren't listening. Good eye contact with the person asking the question is vital during this entire process.

GROUP

This is a screening interview often used when numerous applicants need to be actually seen to determine a candidate's potential. This interview involves you with several other candidates all being interviewed at the same time. The airlines commonly use this type of interview when hiring flight attendants. The purpose is twofold. First, do you meet the physical requirements for the job such as height, weight, physical agility. Next, how comfortable and confident are you in a group situation. As this process looks to determine those with poor communication and interpersonal skills — practice speaking clearly, firmly, and with a friendly tone. Don't be surprised when you get only a couple of opportunities to answer questions. Radiate confidence that you can effectively deal with the demanding public and that you are cool, calm, and collected under high pressure situations. These traits are imperative to doing the job well and this intimidating format seems to aid the employer in a speedy elimination process.

STRESS

These have become less common as employers became more skilled in hiring and recognize there is a need to recruit as well as eliminate. Silence is the stress technique many interviewers commonly use. Silence makes most job hunters nervous and encourages them to babble. When you finish answering the question, quietly tolerate the silence and wait. Not more than 15 seconds will pass before they ask the next question and you will demonstrate your self confidence and professional demeanor, poise, and ability to handle pressure.

There are specific situations intended to put you in the hot seat for the entire interview. Although these are more rare today, let me discuss two scenarios and give you ideas on how to handle each. The first requires two or three interviewers. They begin with rapidly fired questions, allowing little if no time to answer one question before the next one is thrown at you. The IRS has often used this style when interviewing for collectors, auditors, and agents. The correct response is to say "Just a minute here. I do want to answer your questions, so let's start with Tom first and once I've answered his question, then I'll answer George's. Tom, could you repeat your question, please." Regaining control is the only way to not be disqualified as a potential candidate.

The second example rarely happens, but just might. The interviewer walks into the room, sits down, and glares at you. He says "You don't know anything" as he crumples your resume into a ball and throws it on the floor. He waits for your reaction. Commonly, people feel fear, anger, and disgust. This person is demanding and intimidating as he feels the job will require you to deal with demanding people. An appropriate response would be "There is a lot I can learn from you." And see where this leads. Do your best to listen. Demonstrate that you are easy to train, eager to learn. Play to the person's ego. Then once you leave, seriously evaluate if this is a good work environment for you. The dictator will probably use intimidation on the job. This style should raise a serious red flag for you to decide whether you really want to work for this person and their organization.

BREAKFAST/LUNCH/DINNER

Meals often provide a more relaxed atmosphere and candidates often chat, saying things that hurt their candidacy. This is an interview — you are not speaking off the record; all ears are listening to you. Remain in your role and answer each question accordingly. More lengthy answers are OK — but never monopolize the conversation. Be aware of their desire to learn about the *real* you. They also watch your restaurant etiquette. Allow them to pay for the meal. Select an entrée that is easy to eat, not spaghetti or lobster or hand foods. Focus on the conversation. I recommend you never drink alcohol. This is a job interview. If you must drink, nurse something very slowly, leaving it half touched. You need to remain sharp.

These meetings often try to uncover personality traits and outside interests. Are you a good conversationalist? Would you interact well at company functions or client meetings? What are your personal circumstances? Married? Children? Divorced? Time consuming sports?

To control this meeting, ask a lot of questions about the company, the duties of the job, and immediate challenges. Continually sell yourself and your ability to do the job.

VIDEO

This is a rare situation, but it has happened to a couple of my clients and it might happen to you. The company plans to video the entire process. Often this is to "show" management back at headquarters the candidates and eliminate the expense of flying you to that location. Trainers and sales personnel are most likely to be asked to be videotaped. Often a short presentation is required from you as part of this process. You are almost always told in advance about this type of format. Here are some guidelines:

1. Ask in advance all the details about this format. Whom is it for? Where will the camera be? How long? Any special presentations you will be asked to make? Don't expect them to volunteer much, so ask and call back a second time if you need to clarify more about this process.

2. Practice using a video camera to record a role-play session. Your movements and nervous actions are exaggerated on video. Watch for your non-verbal clues and facial expressions.

3. Focus totally on the interviewer and forget the camera. Staring into the camera will just make you nervous and cause you to make mistakes.

4. Exude your poise and self-confidence. There characteristics are being heavily assessed.

5. Smile often — when the tape is viewed, you will come across as a warmer, more likable person.

NEGOTIATION

The job offer has been made. You're now in control. The employer has changed hats and eagerly attempts to get you to join their team. Use this time to learn about the politics, the company's goals and the role your position and decisions play in the global scheme of the company.

Ask about promotional tracks and training opportunities. Ask to meet your potential staff and, if you have not met the person who would be your boss, insist on it before you accept. You should now learn all about their benefits and decide on an agreeable salary.

This interview can be vital to your assessment of the corporate culture. So often people take the job when offered it on the phone. They start and within a week they know they've made a terrible mistake. Often, a negotiations interview would reveal potential conflicts, such as changes in benefits or job duties that were initially mentioned at the first interview. One client was promised an initial training program. At the negotiations interview that promise was changed to be offered six months or so down the line. That training was vital to her success. When a few other things changed also, she passed on the job.

There may be reasons to refuse a job. Ask, "Are there any problems, situations, or reasons that exist that could dissuade me from taking this job?" Never underestimate intense, political conflicts between employees you will manage. Get the facts and think it through thoroughly. Determine the time, energy, and upper management agenda to solve or continue this often emotionally draining situation.

Lastly, ask if there was an internal candidate who did not get this job. Will you supervise that person? How will they react to you? Be concerned about how that candidate's workmates will interact and treat you. Be careful, these situations can often sabotage your ability to succeed in the new position.

Gather your facts, insights, and impressions during this time. Properly utilized, this interview allows you to select an organization where you really can leave each day saying, "I love my job."

9

PITFALLS TO AVOID

Part of our strategy for a successful interview is to have you avoid "mistakes" that many people often make. The fourteen common errors you'll want to avoid are:

1. Arriving late. Many employers feel that if you're late for the interview, you may never show up for your job. Need I say more? Get the directions, know how to get there, and give yourself more than enough time so that you can arrive early. Wait, and collect your thoughts then open the employer's door about five minutes before the interview is to start.

2. Wearing inappropriate attire. Most people simply don't think about their appearance. They don't realize the importance of that first thirty seconds, when they meet the employer for the first time. The employer looks at you, and makes a decision based on your appearance as to whether or not you would fit in their organization. They decide not to hire you based on the way you're dressed. Whether you like it or not, it's human nature and it happens every day. Their immediate decision is based on whether you would be an appropriate person to *represent* their company. Remember, you want to get the job. The interview is not the time to express your creative personality. Many people lose jobs because of their wild clothes, earrings, mismatched colors, out-dated wardrobes, and sloppiness. Put your best foot forward. After all, it is important that the interview *not* end the moment they see you.

Appearance is crucial for people who are in high-visibility positions. You'd be surprised at some of the things I've seen people wear to interview; gaudy make-up, mini-mini skirts, old fashioned polyester suits, the list is endless. There are several books, such as Molloy's on ***Dress for Success***, that have been published on professional appearance. I recommend men wear business suits, navy blue or dark gray have tested well. A white shirt is the best choice. Select a very conservative tie. Women, a business suit, a business coat dress, or a jacket over a skirt, are appropriate. I recommend you not wear pants. You probably know what colors look best on you, but navy blue is always a safe color for an interview suit. Something stylish, but still conservative.

Designate an interview outfit that you know is clean, and that can be worn to any interview on last-minute notice. Be sure your outfit makes a positive impression on people. A good way to test an outfit is to wear it to a meeting, then ask people to comment about your outfit and see what kind of reaction you get. This test will give you the feedback to know whether or not it's an outfit you should wear to an interview. Large department stores have personal shoppers; they can also assist you in getting a professional outfit. But don't try to get too trendy. Most organizations like a conservative look.

3. Not conducting market research. It's amazing to me how many people go to a job interview with no information about the company, no thought about the job that they'll be doing, and no idea as to how they're going to relate their skills to the company's needs. The more "inside information" you can get, the more accurately you're going to be able to phrase your answers to demonstrate how your skills will fill the employer needs. This is effective self-marketing. Spend the time to call contacts, read company literature and learn about the employer's needs to help direct you in properly answering their questions. It's imperative to your success.

4. Making the assumption your résumé will get you the job. Do you believe that the employer diligently, and with a microscope, went through your resumé, and has absorbed every single fact there? In reality, hiring employers often have glanced at the resume when they offered you an interview, and have not looked at it again until the second you're in front of them. Secondly, employers know that good resumes can be purchased.

In fact, it's best to assume your resume will not get you the job. You will be selling your skills throughout the entire interview. Don't say, "Oh, well it's in my résumé." Assume they *haven't read* your resume and say, "I've got ten years of experience in the graphic design field."

5. Believing that the person with the best education, skills and experience will get the job. This is not the case based on my experience as a hiring employer, and on discussions with numerous other employers. Sometimes the person that has the best experience, the best skills and the best education doesn't feel like they'd fit into the organization. They just don't have the right personality, or a cooperative attitude. Employers might have gotten concerned that they are overqualified and will leave too quickly. Whatever the reason, don't assume that top credentials are all it takes to get the job.

6. Failing to prepare. This is a fatal error. I can't expound upon how important it is that you prepare prior to the interview. Write out answers to prospective questions. Analyze and prepare your 5 Point Agenda. Memorize your 60 Second Sell. Practice interview questions, using a role playing situation. Try a tape recorder or get feedback from another person. Advanced preparation makes you feel and sound confident about your abilities to do their job. It's crucial to your success.

7. Assuming the interviewer is an expert. This is a myth. Very few interviewers have hired a lot of people. Most are managers that hire only their own staff. Very few are skillfully trained in techniques on how to conduct an interview. Those that receive any training often just get instructions on which questions are legal to ask. Don't assume that they'll know the direction the interview needs to go. Sometimes it's to your advantage to direct the conversation to effectively make your points.

8. Failing to inspire confidence. Interviews are not the time to be humble and meek. If you don't express confidence and competency that you can do the job, the employer will recognize that you probably *can't* do their job.

9. Failing to demonstrate skills. Many people will sit through the interview, but they don't clearly tell the employer the skills that they'd bring to the job. They're quiet, their answers may be very general, or very vague. Employers don't hire for vague generalities. They hire for specifics. Specific skills, past experience, examples of how you have done that kind of work before. Specifics are what employers make decisions to hire on. Be sure to be detailed, but concise whenever you answer.

10. Appearing desperate or highly stressed out. An unfortunate reality of hiring is that people are desperate. When you're an employer, interviewing with somebody whose desperation keeps coming through often makes you feel sorry for the person, but you don't hire them. I've had many employers tell me, "You know, I really felt sorry for him," but then I asked, "Well, did you hire him?" And they all say, "Well no, I didn't." The desperation turns them off and often makes them question your competency. They're afraid that person doesn't want their particular job, they just want ANY job. And to the employer, you wanting *their* job is what's most important. You want to appear as if there are other opportunities on your horizon. You may have to act, maybe you *are* desperate. But if you transmit that desperation to the employer in the interview, it can hurt your chances of getting hired.

11. Failing to properly complete supplemental questions or tests. Some employers will ask you to fill out additional questionnaires or submit to a test during the hiring process. These must be taken seriously so try to gather as much information as possible in advance to thoroughly prepare. Ask the organization for the specific details on exactly what the tests or written supplemental questions will be about. Don't guess, **know**. I've seen employers give equipment simulation tests, typing tests, computer tests, written exams, personality tests, problems to solve, materials to proofread, work to analyze and prioritize, plus other tasks to determine your hireability. Learn as much as you can and practice in advance. The day of the interview, practice again, then do your best. Most errors come from nerves and being unprepared. Some employers may want you to submit to a drug test. Do so. Your refusal will eliminate you as a candidate. If you take prescription medicine, inform the person conducting the test to document the prescription.

12. Believing that the most important time is the last five minutes. Actually, the most important time is the first thirty seconds, when they at least make the decision that they're going to listen to you. Then take every opportunity to demonstrate your skills and your abilities, with proven examples of work you've done in the past. In reality, using *all* the time is most important.

13. Believing references are all created equal. They are not. Some individuals, especially those who have previously worked with you can aid you in being offered a position. Other times, they can actually deter an employer from hiring you. When choosing references, consider testing them out to learn exactly what they will say about you. Ask a friend to call and get a reference on you. Have that person report back. One client reported that her assistant discussed how the assistant had really organized the office himself and the client came off in a less than favorable light. Needless to say, she dropped that name from her reference list.

Obtain permission from a reference in advance. Help them to be a good reference by writing them a letter and nicely reminding them about the experiences and abilities you'd like them to discuss. This letter often aids in refreshing their memories if it's been awhile since you've worked together.

Under no circumstances use a boss who will say negative things. Find someone else who can talk about your strengths and contributions even if you were fired. After all, you select your references, so choose those names carefully.

14. Assuming your major goal is to get the job. Really? I thought your major goal is to find out about the job, to learn what the company's needs are, and to examine and determine if your skills and abilities fit the company's needs. Would this be a good marriage? Uniting your skills and abilities, their jobs needs, and bringing you both together? That's really what you're looking for. During the interview you are investigating them just like they are investigating you. Realize it's an exchange for both of you to decide if this is a possible fit and a good job for you. Use the time to gather decision making information to aid you in selecting a position in which you'll be able to contribute, be productive, and enjoy going to work.

10

THE SPOTLIGHT IS ON YOU

In every interview you are an actor. Your role is the job seeker. Just as Hollywood's top stars practice and prepare, so will you. Every actor knows that verbal words are enhanced by body language, facial expressions, voice intonations and props. When the job interview's spotlight shines on you, you begin a one-time-only performance. So make your words, body language, voice and props work to aid you in landing the job.

DEALING WITH NERVOUSNESS

Important events where we are judged and need to perform well can make anyone nervous. A little nervousness can actually aid you in being sharp, on your toes, and improve your performance. A heart-thumping, face twitching, voice quivering nervousness will reflect poorly on you and the strong self-confident, "I can solve your problems" impression you are trying to make. Try these techniques to decrease your nervousness.

- **Technique 1.** Visualize success. See yourself smiling and happy. In your mind create a picture of the employer's eyes glued to you, hanging on every word. Hear them say, "I want

71

you for the job." Believe that you will be successful, liked and wanted in this encounter. Your state of mind directly impacts your performance. Focus only on confidence-building thoughts.

■ **Technique 2.** Listen to a motivational tape shortly before the interview. The confidence and morale-boosting words will give you needed moral support and decrease your apprehensions.

■ **Technique 3.** Rid your body of nervous tension. Just before you go into the interview find a private spot outside or in the rest room, and shake each leg. Then shake both arms and hands. The physical exercise releases the tension that has built up and relaxes you.

■ **Technique 4.** Take deep breaths. As your hand reaches for the door, take a couple deep breaths, slowly breathing in and out.

All four techniques will help to decrease your nervousness. And practice makes perfect. All the preparation creating answers, and your 60 Second Sell should reassure you that you are prepared and will do your best.

WHAT TO TAKE

The night before the interview select what you need to take. Always have extra résumés — yes, they do lose them and misplace them. Bring your list of references. Be sure all addresses and phone numbers are current and accurate. Include any work samples and the list of questions you intend to ask. Carry your research, the list of those questioned you've answered, your 5 Point Agenda and 60 Second Sell. You'll want to review all this preparation an hour or two before entering the interview, to keep the ideas fresh in your mind. Include a note pad and pen in case you need them.

Decide if you will carry a briefcase or a simple leather-bound notebook holder into the interview. Organize your materials, and you are ready to go. Be careful to not have too many things — briefcase, note pad binder, materials, purse — all in your hands. Combine and compact things into one easily carried piece, two maximum.

FIRST IMPRESSIONS

First impressions are difficult to change. Before you even say hello, the employer's mind is evaluating attire and style, formulating an opinion, since what you wear sends powerful signals. They must be positive or these could eliminate your chances of getting the job. Select a suit that is conservative, but modern. Be certain it is clean, and pay careful attention to the details. Smile at everyone you meet. As you introduce yourself to the receptionist, smile and take a moment to ask her name. Be sure to add you are glad to meet her. When the interviewer approaches, stand, smile, and offer a firm handshake. Nothing creates a poorer impression than a weak couple of fingers shake. Start out exuding confidence; the smile and firm handshake are key.

NON-VERBAL CLUES

Employers evaluate what they hear, while lending credence to what they see. Nervous gestures such as playing with your wedding ring or tapping your fingers can absorb their attention. Nervous job hunters then compensate with crossing their arms, a gesture that radiates a closed, non approachable, "stay away from me" message. To demonstrate that you are relaxed and confidant sit with your hands on your lap, or rest them open on the table if one is in front of you. Equally acceptable is to open your note pad and have a pen to hold.

Your movements, gestures, posture and facial expressions are an important part of your overall performance. A sincere smile sends a warm, confident message. Eye contact is crucial and conveys that your message is believable. We all get suspicious of a person who focuses eyes on the floor, to the side, but rarely on us. Practice until it is second nature to look *at* the person when answering a question.

Your face can reflect so many expressions — humor, confidence, seriousness, concern, enthusiasm — all of which add depth and meaning to your words. Be sure to not sit there stoic, with a blank face. So often you fail to appear "real" and come across boring and dull. If you sit rigid, upright, or frozen — you communicate anxiety and insincerity. Likewise, slouching projects cowardliness, insecurity, less competence. Sit up tall but lean forward from time to time to make your point and draw in your listener.

Use vocal intonations to make your point. Pauses, soft tones, louder tones, all add interest to a conversation. One CEO commented that she listens to applicants tone. If they are long-winded, monotone and boring, she eliminates them. After all, she is the one who will be constantly listening to them in meetings. She, like many employers, wants someone confident, human, more personable. This does not mean loud and boisterous. Quiet introverts often excel in interviews because they project a quiet, confident self. Be yourself, be natural, but use these nonverbal techniques to project a more appealing image to the employer.

SUPPORT DOCUMENTATION

Proof. Every employer loves to see proof that you can do the job. Just as a graphic designer never interviews without a portfolio of work samples, you need to bring samples that demonstrate your abilities to do the job.

Proof can be a form you have created that sped up production, a spreadsheet that is an efficient tracking system, articles you have written, materials you have created, brochures that list you as a panelist or speaker. Bring anything that clearly demonstrates how you have done the job before. Remember, a picture, or, in this case, a paper, journal, flyer, etc., is worth a thousand words.

FIELD KNOWLEDGE

Employers dread taking time to train people who change careers. If you are changing career fields, be sure to become knowledgeable about the new field. Read books and articles on the new field. Talk with successful people who hold jobs similar to the one you want. Become conversant in the field's jargon, and learn about future trends and needs. Acquire the necessary background to overcome the employer's objection that you know *nothing* about the field.

Job hunters trying to remain in their field, should read about trends, new changes and current problems. They should be nimble and able to discuss the position and the field in which the work is done. They should learn the field's needs, and how, as a product, they can address those needs. They should become well versed in the company's products, services, and operations.

If you educate yourself before the interview, you can present a very appealing package and cross over into new and very different, complex fields or companies. Never go to the interview without doing this important homework.

60 SECOND WORK EXAMPLE

Clearly communicating with an example can paint a picture that allows the employer to see you doing similar tasks, successfully, for them. Predetermined work examples are a very effective part of the tools you bring to the meeting. You'll never flounder and search for an example. Pre-selection allows you to slowly sift through your background and extract the right situation to make your point. Prepare examples that demonstrate each component in your 5 Point Agenda. Prepare examples that deal with problem solving, supervisory style, planning/organization skills, especially if your job deals with projects and deadlines. These examples or stories need to be introduced, told, then summarized in no more than 60 seconds. Advance preparation allows you to introduce these examples where appropriate questions allow.

If asked a question on dealing with employee performance or problems solving, you could try an example like this: "Solving problems is an important part of my work. At Northwest Hospital I had an assistant who was overwhelmed with her regular workload and trying to learn our new WordPerfect software. Everything was getting behind. I sat her down and we talked about the problem. Laura found it very hard to concentrate with any distractions as she applied what she'd been taught in the computer training class. We decided that Laura could spend one hour each day from 4 to 5 p.m. with her door closed and phone forwarded to voice mail for two weeks. We determined specific goals she needed to learn — document editing, mail merges — that were necessary for her to master in order to get the department back up to speed. I encouraged her daily and she did make the needed progress. In fact, she surpassed all my expectations within two months and really improved our paper-flow productivity with her new skills. I think it was the effort I made getting her input and help in finding an acceptable solution that encouraged and motivated her to try harder." When you offer specific details you make the employer think "yes, that's what we need." And you'll go a long way towards being hired.

INCORPORATE TRANSFERABLE SKILLS

Many of your abilities are skills that are valuable from one employer to another. These "transferable skills" build a fuller picture for the employer to consider.

You possess many skills that you fail to recognize, but that an employer will see as necessary and important. For example, computer skills are highly valued from one employer to another. Here are seven skill areas to consider. Select those that are important in doing the employer's job well and incorporate them into your answers and examples.

- **Managerial Skills** — set goals, see big picture, solve problems, handle details, plan projects, analyze, find resources, work well with others, obtain maximum productivity from others, gain cooperation, implement changes, supervise others, plan work flow, mediate staff conflicts, delegate, think globally.

- **Organizational/Planning Skills** — structure events, coordinate people and details, organize tracking or filing systems, set time lines, forecast, determine priorities, manage all aspects of large or multiple projects, develop alternatives, determine resources, solve problems, see the big picture and all the interacting components too, attention to the tiniest details, gather support and cooperation from others.

- **Communication Skills** — public speaker, trainer, teacher, influence others, exchange ideas, use probing questions to determine needs of others, sell products/services/ideas, persuade others to do what you want, use humor, tell stories, entertain others, write messages that clearly get across your meaning, make impassioned pleas, edit comprehensive reports/proposals, express creativity, use vocabulary/grammar/language skills effectively, write articles, edit reports/publications.

- **Leadership Skills** — lead groups, motivate others, cause change, activist, decision maker, visionary, forecaster, recognize opportunities, praise others, direct projects and individuals.

- **Financial Skills** — manage budgets, create cost spreadsheets, do price comparisons, negotiate better deals, notice cost cutting or profit making opportunities, oversee cash management, use charts/graphs to make points, be financially resourceful.

- **Analytical Skills** — research, analyze data, interpret results, organize large volumes of information, evaluate options considering pros/cons and consequences, design efficient systems, collect and process information in user friendly form, diagnose problems, determine workable solutions, seek more efficient procedures, produce technical reports/surveys or questionnaires, investigate, make new discoveries, implement new systems, test new ideas/processes/procedures/systems .

- **Interpersonal Skills** — counsel, conduct negotiations, listen, be empathetic, be sensitive to others, build rapport, deal effectively with conflicts, interact socially, help others, share ideas, solve problems, mediate, bring people together.

HANDLING SMALL EMPLOYERS

In the next decade, according to the Department of Labor, job growth will increase by the greatest degree with small employers, particularly organizations with fewer than 100 people. This presents a dilemma to you as often very little information about the employer is available prior to the interview. To aid you in your preparation, try to obtain as much information from the person who arranges the interview or try someone else in the office. Call and ask a few questions. If you get "Oh, they'll cover that," you'll need to use your best guess and prepare. As you start the interview, if you employ this technique, you can gain the necessary information and reorganize your answers to address their spoken needs. Simply say "Mr. Employer, before we get started, could you tell me in more detail about the day-to-day responsibilities?" Then ask "What do you consider the priorities?" "Any special training or experience to be successful in the job?"

From those few questions, you've learned the important ingredients this employer desires. You can re-address their needs by quickly editing your 60 Second Sell. You may need to adapt quickly, but you've gotten the insights and can now stress your strengths to answer their needs, when most other candidates will be operating blind.

LISTENING

Hear their questions, *hear* their needs, *hear* their expectations. If you listen carefully, employers often reveal everything you need to know.

So often job hunters just don't listen. It is frustrating to the interviewer to ask questions that never get answered. So listen closely. Many employers reveal their "hidden agendas," those few things that really influence their decision if you listen closely to the questions they ask and the information they offer. I recently interviewed five people to hire a program coordinator. I told each candidate that computer skills were important. One person emphasized her organizational abilities, another her attention to detail and willingness to do whatever was asked. A third repeatedly discussed her WordPerfect abilities, never drawing comparisons to the revealed fact that this employer's software was Microsoft Word. The hired gentleman spoke of computer abilities and brought sample flyers, documents and even a newsletter he'd done. He met my most important criteria — computer skills. The others never heard me. As the potential employer, I told them, but they didn't listen. If they had, they might have been the one who got the job. Instead, he did!

11

THE CONVINCING CLOSE

Most employers use some sort of rating system at the end of an interview. Some may just jot down notes, others use a comprehensive evaluation form. With this in mind, how you end the interview will be a vital component in securing the job offer.

WHAT EMPLOYERS REMEMBER

Most seasoned interviewers will tell you that it is easy to forget a person 60 seconds after they run out the door. You can often sit back at the end of the day, look at the resumes and wonder who was who.

Using the 60 Second Sell and the 5 Point Agenda ensures repetition of your major strengths. Creating examples that demonstrate these strengths, plus effectively answering questions in less than 60 seconds will reinforce your abilities and desire to do the job. Using your 60 Second Sell as you are ending the interview will leave the employer with those few thoughts to ponder as they fill out their evaluation form, remembering your five most marketable skills to meet their needs and do their job.

The end has come, they have asked all their questions, you've followed with yours. You've learned about the next stage and when they will be making a decision. Just before you get up to leave, end with your closing 60 Second Sell. With a little adaptation, it might sound like this:

> Thank you for the opportunity to meet with you and learn about your needs for an Executive Director. I believe my 13 years in association management, assisting associations in their development and growth would be an asset to you. It sounds like I'd be able to put to use all the event planning and the media contacts I've developed to create very profitable events, obtaining the needed publicity and corporate sponsors that ensure high attendance. I believe the addition of seminars and workshops would be a new revenue source for you, as it was for my last employer. Finally, I think my resourcefulness to be innovative, maximize the use of volunteers, and work with restricted budgets would be very beneficial in achieving your goals. I believe I would make some very valuable contributions if I join your team. Thank you again for this meeting.

Format the close to directly apply your abilities to what they have revealed about the position. Once said, stand, shake hands, and leave.

EMPLOYER RATING CHART

As soon as the door closes, the employer takes notes. She decides whether or not you are someone they could work with. Below is a typical ratings report an employer might complete after each interview. Note that this employer uses facts and impressions they've gathered during the interview process. First the determination — can you do the job — evaluating technical competency. Noting weaknesses and strengths. Skill areas are examined; job knowledge, communication skills, managerial style, organizational/planning problem solving and decision-making abilities are rated. A decision is made whether you are a potential candidate to be hired for the job.

INTERVIEW EVALUATION

Name:_____

Position:_____

Technical Competency
Candidate's strongest skills are:

1. _____

2. _____

3. _____

Compared to our job needs, these strengths are:
☐ Not Important ☐ Somewhat Important ☐ Important

Previous job performance of technical skills
☐ Poor ☐ Below Average ☐ Adequate ☐ Good ☐ Excellent

Weakness or area of concern: _____

_____

Overall Job Knowledge:
☐ Poor ☐ Below Average ☐ Adequate ☐ Good ☐ Excellent

Oral Communication Skills:
☐ Poor ☐ Below Average ☐ Adequate ☐ Good ☐ Excellent

Written Communication Skills:
☐ Poor ☐ Below Average ☐ Adequate ☐ Good ☐ Excellent

Organizational/Planning Abilities:
☐ Poor ☐ Below Average ☐ Adequate ☐ Good ☐ Excellent

Managerial Skills:
Describe candidate's supervisory style: _____

_____

Rate style in relation to managing employees who will report to this person:
☐ Poor ☐ Fair ☐ Good ☐ Excellent

Computer Skills:
Hardware experience: _____
Software experience: _____
Training needed: _____

Decision Making Experience:
☐ Below Average ☐ Adequate ☐ Good ☐ Excellent

Interpersonal/Customer Skills
☐ Poor ☐ Fair ☐ Average ☐ Good ☐ Excellent

Analytical Abilities:
☐ Undetermined ☐ Poor ☐ Fair ☐ Good ☐ Excellent

Work Ethic:
☐ Undetermined ☐ Poor ☐ Fair ☐ Good ☐ Excellent

Personality:
Describe:_____
_____

Asset for the Job:
☐ Yes ☐ No ☐ Most Definitely

Comments:_____
_____

Hiring Rating:
☐ Definitely not ☐ Adequate with some reservations
☐ Possible hire ☐ Definitely hire

Signature: _____ Date: _____

POST INTERVIEW ASSESSMENT

Immediately after the interview, find a spot to sit down and write out your assessment of the employer and the position. This will aid you to improve your interviews in the future, to evaluate the employer's needs for future interviews if the process continues, and note any special problems or tough questions to practice answering in the future. Jot down these thoughts:

- Describe job duties
- Impression of the potential workplace
- Impression of future boss
- Concerns or weak areas you might have in performing this job
- Training time to get up to speed
- Unanswered questions or concerns you'll need further clarification on
- Tough questions you found hard to answer
- Rate your performance
- Note any areas where you might try to improve
- Are you interested in this job? company?

THANK YOU NOTES

Employers can be influenced once you have walked out the door. A thank you note that arrives can often reaffirm they have made the right choice. The note can tip the hand in your favor if it is between you and someone else. The employer believes a person who really wants the job is likely to perform better on the job. Your note should be a note card with the words "thank you" grazing the card's opening page in a professional business-like style. These are available in the local drug store or card shop. Jot down a few lines, thanking them for the opportunity and reiterating a strength or two you would bring as a "valuable contributor to their team." Often, seminar students object, saying "Shouldn't I send a letter?" Letters will not have the impact. Sometimes they are opened by an assistant and not seen. Other times, they are only glanced at. The notes — handwritten (print if your writing is not legible) — is a *personal* communication. Demonstrate the extra effort you put into your work. It certainly won't negatively impact your chances. It's important to note that most candidates *do not* send thank you notes. Here again is the chance to move to the top and be reevaluated. Notes must be mailed within 24 hours, preferably the same day as the interview if timing allows.

HOW TO REMAIN A VIABLE CANDIDATE WHEN SOMEONE ELSE GETS THE JOB

Ten to twenty percent of all new hires do not work out. The reasons vary — the candidate continued interviewing and got a better offer or their performance and personality did not fit the employer's needs.

One candidate accepted a position for a top management position. Relocation was involved so the employer agreed to wait eight weeks for the candidate to start. On the night before he was scheduled to start, a fax arrived saying the person had changed his mind and wasn't coming.

There are times when follow up can win you the job. Here's what to do:

1. Call to determine why the employer selected another. Reiterate that you are still interested in the job if the person doesn't work out, tell the employer to then reconsider you. I recommend you not ask why you weren't selected just say you understand. Don't burden the employer with questions on what you did wrong — they are not likely to honestly share that information. And never argue or get defensive. The employer will hire the person they felt was best suited for the job. Probe to learn if the company has any other available positions you might be qualified for. If so, secure the name of the hiring manager and contact that person at once.

2. Check back in four to six weeks to see if the person is working out. If they aren't, the employer will be very glad to hear from you.

3. When you are not the first choice, ask about the other person's skill and experience with a couple of probing questions. "I understand the person had more experience — in what areas?" Asking nicely in a "help me out so I'll improve approach" can allow you to see where your answers and responses need work in the future. If you feel the employer missed some important aspect of your background you can add "I recognize that I was a little

nervous during the interview and probably didn't communicate to you very well my experience in _____ " (you fill in the blank). Then offer solid examples of this experience. If the employer shows interest, ask to come in and meet with them again — anytime, any place.

4. Forget your pride. Pride does not pay your bills. Perhaps you didn't get the initial offer because you didn't sell yourself as effectively as you could have. Whether you are second, third, or fifth choice — it does not matter if in the end you're the one who *takes* the job and goes home with the paycheck. Be humble if you are called back and resell the employer on your abilities to do their job well.

You will not salvage every lost opportunity. But so few candidates ever practice good follow up techniques that you will be among little competition if you do. And under the right circumstances *you* will grab the job from the jaws of defeat and land the position you really want.

12

60 SECONDS &
YOU'RE HIRED

Real people use these techniques everyday. They report that the 60 Second Sell and the 5 Point Agenda were instrumental in landing the job, yet easy to create and use. They refer to them as great hiring shortcuts. Seminar participants sigh with relief once they learn my strategies to handle tricky, tough questions using effective, concise answers. Clients repeatedly secure more money when they apply my salary negotiation guidelines. Hundreds and hundreds have used these strategies and they all had the same conclusion — they really work. That's why I'm convinced these strategies will work for you.

Let me share a few success stories. No, not the easy cases — I selected the hard ones, those with real life challenges that you could also be facing, to prove these techniques *land* jobs. Our real people include:

Tom —   A laid off, highly paid senior executive

Patricia —   A financial executive who wanted to change fields

Jeff —   A new college grad, facing the worst job market in 30 years

Linda —   Handling a divorce and a job change

Don —   Who wanted to change careers at 41

Mary —   An association director who was fired

Tom was a talented Chief Financial Officer who had been highly paid before his company sold the broadcasting business whose financial operations he oversaw. Headhunters had told Tom he was overpaid and needed to expect a $20,000 salary cut. Tom's resume and targeted cover letter got him an interview with one of the country's top communication companies. This employer conducted nine hours of interviews with Tom over several meetings. Tom felt that the 5 Point Agenda helped him to demonstrate his abilities beyond his financial skills to include his team development, strategic planning, and presentation abilities. The short 60 second answers really got the conversations going. He landed the job, got a better salary package than he had before by using our negotiations guidelines. Within one year Tom was promoted to Vice President of Finance.

Patricia wanted to change fields. She was fascinated with software development, but all her controller experience had been in retail apparel. She spent hours researching this new field. She wrote to say it was her 60 Second Sell and my advice on answering tough questions that helped her to land her dream job. She's now happily the controller for a growing software company.

Jeff found that a business degree from a good four year college was not as marketable as he thought it would be. On graduation day no one was standing in line to hire him. He was discouraged at how difficult and how long the job hunt was taking. He had worked construction jobs to help pay for his college education and thus had no applicable experience to land his goal — a position in store management. Jeff and I worked on creating a 5 Point Agenda and 60 Second Sell that demonstrated his strong work ethic and his ability to work well with all kinds of people. He was amazed that he indeed had important skills to sell an employer. He worked hard developing great answers to the potential questions. Jeff was hired as an Assistant Store Manager for a national paint store. His years in construction helped him to excel in his new career — selling house paint.

Linda was going through a difficult divorce when she got a notice that her employer was closing the branch office where she worked. Her situation was desperate — as sole support of her children she needed a job. Linda had had ten interviews and had failed miserably at each before I met her.

Linda and I evaluated her strengths. She'd never heard of such innovative techniques as the 5 Point Agenda or the 60 Second Sell. We created these hiring strategies and also worked on answers to difficult questions. After two tries, Linda was hired as a Loan Officer with one of

America's top banks.

Don was 41 and hated the high pressured finance world. He lost two jobs in corporate restructurings and he spent ten months looking for a finance job he didn't want after his last layoff.

Our sessions focused on changing his belief that at 41 he could not enter the retail merchandising world. He was willing to take a salary cut and tried a part-time retail job before officially launching a full scale job hunt. Together we worked hard to create a 5 Point Agenda and an influential 60 Second Sell. Our sessions of role playing answers to questions using the 60 second approach increased his confidence. Don's new job is in New York City as part of Macy's merchandising buying team.

Mary underestimated how difficult her job search would be when she was fired. She bombed during her first interview, easily tripping over the "Why were you let go" questions. Mary secretly worried if she was as good as she thought. She feared landing a new position that would also have the type of difficult politics that had been her downfall in her last job. We analyzed Mary's strengths as an association executive director — media, PR, events, conferences, interpersonal abilities, organization, and planning. Her weaknesses were budgets, finance and trying to please everyone, especially board members with opposing agendas. Our interview sessions restored her self confidence — I knew she would work again and often told her so. We created a 5 Point Agenda and 60 Second Sell that emphasized her strengths. She investigated the associations to learn which environments offered opportunities to use her strengths, while not relying on her to provide the financial direction she was not skilled at. Lastly, she sought an organization with only one boss where she could achieve the goals that one person set out. She felt that using my techniques allowed her to be selected from 155 candidates. She's been very successful (and happy) in her new executive director position.

I've shared my shortcuts and hiring strategies to aid you in communicating to employers how you can meet their needs. There lies the key to open your door of opportunity. Just as Mary, Jeff and countless others have found good positions, so will you. The 5 Point Agenda is an easy tool to create. It provides you with a clear direction to stress your five major strengths, demonstrating how well you can do the employer's job. The 60 Second Sell is a clever strategy that effectively markets your most important abilities in a short, concise way. You can now write out your answers that, once spoken, will convince the employer to hire you. You know exactly how to negotiate for more salary and benefits in a way that produces results. All you need to do now is put these techniques into

action. You too can and will succeed. I know it's just 60 Seconds and
you're hired.

ABOUT THE AUTHOR

Robin Ryan is a nationally recognized authority on job search and hiring. She appears on Seattle's KIRO TV *News at Noon* and KIRO Radio *Money Advice*.

A licensed Vocational Counselor with sixteen years in the Career Development field, she holds a Master's Degree in Counseling and Education from Suffolk University and a Bachelor's Degree in Sociology from Boston College. Robin has established three career centers.

While Director of Counseling Services at the University of Washington, Robin established a corporate recruiting program with Fortune 500 companies including: Mobil, Merck, 3M, Chevron and Proctor & Gamble. With ten years of hiring responsibility, she teaches hiring seminars to employers.

Robin has a private career counseling practice in the Seattle suburb of Renton. She has personally assisted three thousand individuals in their career transition.

Each year thousands of job hunters across the country attend Robin's seminars on job search, resume writing, and interview techniques. She frequently speaks at career fairs, conferences, colleges and association meetings.

Her company, Ryan Consulting and Training offers complete outplacement services to companies in transition. They have worked with numerous large and small companies, non-profits and governmental agencies.

Robin publishes the *Hidden Job Market* quarterly newsletter and is the author of *Job Search Organizer: Everything You Need to Land Your Next Job Faster.*

LET ME KNOW
WHEN YOU SUCCEED

I care about your success. Let me hear how my techniques have helped you land the job you want. You can write to me at:

Robin Ryan
Ryan Consulting and Training
PO Box 40150
Bellevue, WA 98015-4150

INDEX

CAREER
RESOURCES

Contact Impact Publications to receive a free copy of their latest comprehensive and annotated catalog of over 2,000 career resources (books, subscriptions, training programs, videos, audiocassettes, computer software, and CD-ROM).

The following career resources are available directly from Impact Publications. Complete the following form or list the titles, include postage (see formula at the end), enclose payment, and send your order along with your name and address to:

IMPACT PUBLICATIONS
9104-N Manassas Drive
Manassas Park, VA 22111
Tel. 703/361-7300
FAX 703/335-9486

Orders from individuals must be prepaid by check, moneyorder, Visa or MasterCard number. We accept telephone and FAX orders with a Visa or MasterCard number.

Qty.	TITLES	Price	TOTAL
INTERVIEWS, NETWORKING & SALARY NEGOTIATIONS			
___	60 Seconds and You're Hired!	$9.95	_____
___	Dynamite Answers to Interview Questions	$10.95	_____
___	Dynamite Salary Negotiation	$12.95	_____
___	Great Connections	$11.95	_____
___	How to Work a Room	$9.95	_____
___	Interview for Success	$11.95	_____
___	New Network Your Way to Job and Career Success	$12.95	_____

97

___ The Secrets of Savvy Networking $11.99   _____
___ Sweaty Palms $9.95   _____

RESUMES AND LETTERS

___ 200 Letters for Job Hunters $17.95   _____
___ Dynamite Cover Letters $10.95   _____
___ Dynamite Resumes $10.95   _____
___ Electronic Resume Revolution $12.95   _____
___ Electronic Resumes for the New Job Market $11.95   _____
___ High Impact Resumes and Letters $12.95   _____
___ Job Search Letters That Get Results $12.95   _____
___ The Resume Catalog $15.95   _____
___ Resumes for Re-Entry: A Woman's Handbook $10.95   _____

SKILLS, TESTING, SELF-ASSESSMENT, EMPOWERMENT

___ 7 Habits of Highly Effective People $11.00   _____
___ Discover the Best Jobs for You $11.95   _____
___ Do What You Are $14.95   _____
___ Do What You Love, the Money Will Follow $10.95   _____
___ Finding the Hat That Fits $10.00   _____
___ Stop Postponing the Rest of Your Life $9.95   _____
___ What Color Is Your Parachute? $14.95   _____
___ Where Do I Go From Here With My Life? $10.95   _____
___ Wishcraft $10.95   _____

DRESS, APPEARANCE, IMAGE

___ John Molloy's New Dress for Success (men) $10.95   _____
___ Red Socks Don't Work! (men) $14.95   _____
___ The Winning Image $17.95   _____
___ Women's Dress for Success $9.95   _____

JOB SEARCH STRATEGIES AND TACTICS

___ 40+ Job Hunting Guide $23.95   _____
___ 110 Biggest Mistakes Job Hunters Make $14.95   _____
___ Change Your Job, Change Your Life $14.95   _____
___ Complete Job Finder's Guide to the 90s $13.95   _____
___ Complete Job Search Handbook $12.95   _____
___ Cracking the Over-50 Job Market $11.95   _____
___ Dynamite Tele-Search $10.95   _____
___ Electronic Job Search Revolution $12.95   _____
___ Five Secrets to Finding a Job $12.95   _____
___ Go Hire Yourself an Employer $9.95   _____
___ Guerrilla Tactics in the New Job Market $5.99   _____
___ How to Get Interviews From Classified Job Ads $14.95   _____
___ Job Hunting After 50 $12.95   _____
___ Joyce Lain Kennedy's Career Book $29.95   _____
___ Knock 'Em Dead $19.95   _____
___ Professional's Job Finder $18.95   _____
___ Right Place At the Right Time $11.95   _____
___ Rites of Passage At $100,000+ $29.95   _____

___ Super Job Search $22.95 ___
___ Who's Hiring Who $9.95 ___
___ Work in the New Economy $14.95 ___

BEST JOBS AND EMPLOYERS FOR THE 90s

___ 100 Best Companies to Work for in America $27.95 ___
___ 100 Best Jobs for the 1990s and Beyond $19.95 ___
___ 101 Careers $12.95 ___
___ American Almanac of Jobs and Salaries $17.00 ___
___ America's 50 Fastest Growing Jobs $9.95 ___
___ America's Fastest Growing Employers $14.95 ___
___ Best Jobs for the 1990s and Into the 21st Century $12.95 ___
___ Hoover's Handbook of American Business (annual) $34.95 ___
___ Hoover's Handbook of World Business (annual) $32.95 ___
___ Job Seeker's Guide to 1000 Top Employers $22.95 ___
___ Jobs! What They Are, Where They Are, What They Pay $13.95 ___
___ Jobs 1994 $15.95 ___
___ New Emerging Careers $14.95 ___
___ Top Professions $10.95 ___
___ Where the Jobs Are $15.95 ___

KEY DIRECTORIES

___ American Salaries and Wages Survey $94.95 ___
___ Career Training Sourcebook $24.95 ___
___ Careers Encyclopedia $39.95 ___
___ Complete Guide for Occupational Exploration $29.95 ___
___ Dictionary of Occupational Titles $39.95 ___
___ Directory of Executive Recruiters (annual) $39.95 ___
___ Directory of Outplacement Firms $74.95 ___
___ Directory of Special Programs for Minority
     Group Members $31.95
___ Encyclopedia of Careers and Vocational Guidance $129.95
___ Enhanced Guide for Occupational Exploration $29.95
___ Government Directory of Addresses and
     Telephone Numbers $99.95
___ Hoover's Handbook of American Business $34.95
___ Internships (annual) $29.95
___ Job Bank Guide to Employment Services (annual) $149.95
___ Job Hunter's Sourcebook $59.95
___ Moving and Relocation Directory $149.00
___ National Directory of Addresses & Telephone Numbers $129.95
___ National Job Bank (annual) $249.95
___ National Trade and Professional Associations $79.95
___ Minority Organizations $49.95
___ Occupational Outlook Handbook $22.95
___ Personnel Executives Contactbook $149.00
___ Places Rated Almanac $21.95
___ Professional Careers Sourcebook $79.95

INTERNATIONAL, OVERSEAS, AND TRAVEL JOBS

___ Almanac of International Jobs and Careers	$19.95	_____
___ Complete Guide to International Jobs & Careers	$13.95	_____
___ Flying High in Travel	$16.95	_____
___ Guide to Careers in World Affairs	$14.95	_____
___ How to Get a Job in Europe	$17.95	_____
___ How to Get a Job in the Pacific Rim	$17.95	_____
___ Jobs for People Who Love Travel	$12.95	_____
___ Jobs in Paradise	$12.95	_____
___ Jobs in Russia and the Newly Independent States	$15.95	_____
___ Teaching English Abroad	$15.95	_____
___ Work Your Way Around the World	$17.95	_____

PUBLIC-ORIENTED CAREERS

___ Almanac of American Government Jobs and Careers	$14.95	_____
___ Complete Guide to Public Employment	$19.95	_____
___ Federal Jobs in Law Enforcement	$15.95	_____
___ Find a Federal Job Fast!	$13.95	_____
___ Government Job Finder	$14.95	_____
___ Jobs and Careers With Nonprofit Organizations	$14.95	_____
___ How to Get a Federal Job	$15.00	_____
___ Non-Profit's Job Finder	$16.95	_____
___ The Right SF 171 Writer	$19.95	_____

COMPUTER SOFTWARE

___ JOBHUNT™ Quick and Easy Employer Contacts	$49.95	_____
___ INSTANT™ Job Hunting Letters	$39.95	_____
___ ResumeMaker	$49.95	_____
___ Ultimate Job Finder	$59.95	_____

VIDEOS

___ Dialing for Jobs	$129.00	_____
___ Find the Job You Want...and Get It! (4 videos)	$229.95	_____
___ How to Present a Professional Image (2 videos)	$149.95	_____
___ Inside Secrets of Interviewing	$39.95	_____
___ Insider's Guide to Competitive Interviewing	$59.95	_____
___ Networking Your Way to Success	$89.95	_____
___ Very Quick Job Search	$129.00	_____
___ Winning at Job Hunting in the 90s	$89.95	_____

JOB LISTINGS & VACANCY ANNOUNCEMENTS

___ Community (Nonprofit) Jobs (1 year)	$69.00	_____
___ Federal Career Opportunities (6 biweekly issues)	$39.00	_____
___ International Employment Gazette (6 biweekly issues)	$35.00	_____
___ The Search Bulletin (6 issues)	$97.00	_____

MILITARY

___ America's Top Military Careers	$19.95	_____
___ Beyond the Uniform	$12.95	_____
___ Civilian Career Guide	$12.95	_____
___ Does Your Resume Wear Combat Boots?	$9.95	_____
___ From Army Green to Corporate Gray	$15.95	_____
___ Job Search: Marketing Your Military Experience	$14.95	_____
___ Re-Entry	$13.95	_____
___ Retiring From the Military	$22.95	_____

WOMEN AND SPOUSES

___ Balancing Career and Family	$7.95	_____
___ Congratulations: You've Been Fired!	$8.95	_____
___ Doing It All Isn't Everything	$19.95	_____
___ Female Advantage	$19.95	_____
___ New Relocating Spouse's Guide to Employment	$14.95	_____
___ Resumes for Re-Entry: A Handbook for Women	$10.95	_____
___ Smart Woman's Guide to Resumes and Job Hunting	$9.95	_____
___ Survival Guide for Women	$16.95	_____
___ Women's Job Search Handbook	$12.95	_____

MINORITIES AND DISABLED

___ Best Companies for Minorities	$12.00	_____
___ Directory of Special Programs for Minority Group Members	$31.95	_____
___ Job Strategies for People With Disabilities	$14.95	_____
___ Minority Organizations	$49.95	_____
___ Work, Sister, Work	$19.95	_____

COLLEGE STUDENTS

___ 150 Best Companies for Liberal Arts Grads	$12.95	_____
___ Career Planning and Development for College Students and Recent Graduates	$17.95	_____
___ Careers for College Majors	$29.95	_____
___ College Majors and Careers	$15.95	_____
___ Complete Resume and Job Search Book for College Students	$9.95	_____
___ Graduating to the 9-5 World	$11.95	_____
___ How You Really Get Hired	$11.00	_____
___ Kiplinger's Career Starter	$10.95	_____
___ Liberal Arts Jobs	$10.95	_____

ENTREPRENEURSHIP AND SELF-EMPLOYMENT

___ 101 Best Businesses to Start	$15.00	_____
___ 184 Businesses Anyone Can Start	$12.95	_____
___ Best Home-Based Businesses for the 90s	$10.95	_____
___ Entrepreneur's Guide to Starting a Successful Business	$16.95	_____
___ Have You Got What It Takes?	$12.95	_____

___ How to Start, Run, and Stay in Business	$12.95	_____
___ Kiplinger's Working for Yourself	$13.95	_____
___ Mid-Career Entrepreneur	$17.95	_____
___ When Friday Isn't Payday	$12.99	_____

SUBTOTAL _____

Virginia residents add 4½% sales tax _____

POSTAGE/HANDLING ($4.00 for first
title and $1.00 for each additional book) $4.00

Number of additional titles x $1.00 ---------- _____

TOTAL ENCLOSED ----------------_____

SHIP TO:

NAME _____

ADDRESS _____

_____

_____

[ ] I enclose check/moneyorder for $ _____ made
payable to IMPACT PUBLICATIONS.

[ ] Please charge $ _____ to my credit card:

Card # _____

Expiration date: _____/_____

Signature _____